Cambridge Primary
English
Second Edition

Learner's Book 1

Sarah Snashall
Series editors:
Christine Chen
Lindsay Pickton

Boost

HODDER
EDUCATION
AN HACHETTE UK COMPANY

Registered Cambridge International Schools benefit from high-quality programmes, assessments and a wide range of support so that teachers can effectively deliver Cambridge Primary. Visit www.cambridgeinternational.org/primary to find out more.

Third-party websites, publications and resources referred to in this publication have not been endorsed by Cambridge Assessment International Education.

The audio files are free to download at: www.hoddereducation.com/cambridgeextras

Acknowledgements

The Publishers would like to thank the following for permission to reproduce copyright material. Every effort has been made to trace or contact all copyright holders, but if any have been inadvertently overlooked the Publishers will be pleased to make the necessary arrangements at the first opportunity.

Text acknowledgements

pp. 6, 9, 12, 16, 19, 21, 51 © Rosemary Licciardi; **p. 54** © First published by The School Magazine, New South Wales Department of Education; **p. 59** © My Village Gecko Press; **pp. 70–71, 74** *Year Full of Stories*, written by Angela McAllister and illustrated by Christopher Corr, published by Frances Lincoln Children's Books, an imprint of The Quarto Group, copyright © 2016. Reproduced by permission of Quarto Publishing Plc. **p. 102** © By Sigbjørn Obstfelder, translated by Sarah Jane Hails; **p. 104** © Ron Simmons; **p. 108** © 'The Dragonfly' by Eleanor Farjeon from *Blackbird has spoken*, Macmillan; **p. 109** © 2005 by Jodi Simpson. Reprinted by permission of Scholastic Inc.; **p. 110** 'Hush Now' by Mike Barfield; **p. 113** Excerpt from 'Suzie Bitner Was Afraid of the Drain' by Barbara Vance; **pp. 119–123** © text/illustrations from *NOT SO FAST, SONGOLOLO* by Niki Daly. Copyright © 1985 by Niki Daly. Reprinted with the permission of Margaret K. McElderry Books, an imprint of Simon & Schuster Children's Publishing Division. All rights reserved; **p. 121** Reproduced with kind permission of Niki Daly. © Niki Daly; **pp. 125–126** *Shark in the Park*, © Nick Sharratt, published by Corgi UK; **pp. 130–131** *Mr Gumpy's Outing*, © John Burningham (1936–2019), published by Henry Holt & Co.; **pp. 133–138** © Tom Percival, 2018, *Ruby's Worry*, Bloomsbury Publishing Plc.; **pp. 139–140** *Katie Morag's Island Stories*, © Mairi Hedderwick, published by Bodley Head (London, England), 1995; **p. 144** Reproduced with kind permission of Prithviraj Shirole © Prithviraj Shirole; **p. 149** 'Crocodile' by Giles Andreae from *Rumble in the Jungle* by Giles Andreae. Text copyright © 1998 Giles Andreae. Reproduced with kind permission of Coolabi Group Limited; **p. 152** © Coral Rumble.

* Illustrations on pages 70–76 are not by Christopher Corr.

Photo acknowledgements

p. 4 *cc*, **p. 118** *br* © Ourson/Adobe Stock Photo; **p. 11** © Hachette; **p. 18** *br* © Roman Stetsyk/Adobe Stock Photo; **p. 20** *br* © Anastasiya/Adobe Stock Photo; **p. 24** *br* © Bence Sibalin/Shutterstock.com; **p. 31** *cl* © Odua Images/Adobe Stock Photo; **p. 31** *cc* © Vanessa Bentley/Shutterstock.com; **p. 31** *cr* © LM Spencer/Adobe Stock Photo; **p. 31** *cr* © P Calapre/Adobe Stock Photo; **p. 35** *tr* © Anna Kucherova/Adobe Stock Photo; **p. 35** *cl, cr* © Arty U Studio/Adobe Stock Photo; **p. 35** *bl, bc*, **p. 129** *cl, cr* © Jim Cumming 88/Adobe Stock Photo; **p. 35** © Eric Isselée/Adobe Stock Photo; **p. 38** *cl* © Cody/Adobe Stock Photo; **p. 38** *cc* © Ondre J Prosicky/Adobe Stock Photo; **p. 38** *cr* © Jesper/Adobe Stock Photo; **p. 42** *tr* © Ljupco Smokovski/Adobe Stock Photo; **p. 43** *cr* © Gelpi/Adobe Stock Photo; **p. 44** *tr* © Patrick Foto/Adobe Stock Photo; **p. 44** *br* © Patrick Foto/Adobe Stock Photo; **p. 46** *cr* © Sudo Woodo/Adobe Stock Photo; **p. 50** *cr* © Press Master/Adobe Stock Photo; **p. 53** *cl* © Mirecca/Adobe Stock Photo; **p. 53** *cc* © Eremin/Adobe Stock Photo; **p. 53** *cr* © Lucky Photo/Adobe Stock Photo; **p. 56** *b* © R Vika/Adobe Stock Photo; **p. 57** *tl* © Sergey Nivens/Adobe Stock Photo; **p. 57** *br* © Nina Fedorova/Adobe Stock Photo; **p. 58** *tr* © Rasica/Adobe Stock Photo; **p. 60** *cc* © Viki Vector.Adobe Stock Photo; **p. 61** *cc* © Monkey Business/Adobe Stock Photo; **p. 63** *tl* © PX Axe/Adobe Stock Photo; **p. 63** *cl* © Cyno Club/Adobe Stock Photo; **p. 63** *cl* © Veresovich/Adobe Stock Photo; **p. 63** *cl* © Unpict/Shutterstock.com; **p. 63** *cl* © Frenta/Adobe Stock Photo; **p. 66** *br* © Akkharat J/Adobe Stock Photo; **p. 70** *cr* © Nearbirds/Adobe Stock Photo; **p. 75** *cr* © Matis 75/Adobe Stock Photo; **p. 76** *br* © Rash Misingh/Adobe Stock Photo; **p. 83** *bl* © Андрей Глущенко/Adobe Stock Photo; **p. 83** *br* © Pik Selstock/Shutterstock.com; **p. 84** *tr* © Oksana Kuzmina/Adobe Stock Photo; **p. 85** *br* © Spass/Adobe Stock Photo; **p. 89** *br* © Fine Art/Contributor/Getty Images; **p. 91** *cr* © Lightfield Studios/Adobe Stock Photo; **p. 92** *br* © Itestro/Adobe Stock Photo; **p. 93** *br* © Kraken Images.com/Adobe Stock Photo; **p. 96** *cr* © Katrin Timoff/Adobe Stock Photo; **p. 96** *b* © V Voe/Adobe Stock Photo; **p. 97** *cc* © Becky Stares/Shutterstock.com; **p. 98** *tr* © Zakharov Evgeniy/Adobe Stock Photo; **p. 98** *cc* © Ruth Black/Adobe Stock Photo; **p. 98** *cc* © Rangizzzz/Adobe Stock Photo; **p. 98** *bc* © Graham/Adobe Stock Photo; **p. 98** *br* © Larysa Vasylenko/Shutterstock.com; **p. 99** *cc* © Ruth Black/Adobe Stock Photo; **p. 101** *cr* © Xiaoliangge/Adobe Stock Photo; **p. 103** *cc* © Jenko Ataman/Adobe Stock Photo; **p. 104** *cr* © Zilvergolf/Adobe Stock Photo; **p. 105** *cr* © Yliv Design/Adobe Stock Photo; **p. 106** *cr* © Lynnea/Adobe Stock Photo; **p. 107** *cl* © Leekris/Adobe Stock Photo; **p. 107** *tr* © Zdenar Adamsen/Adobe Stock Photo; **p. 107** *bl* © Subbotina Anna/Adobe Stock Photo; **p. 108** *tr* © Rainer Fuhrmann/Adobe Stock Photo; **p. 110** © Sergey Novikov/Adobe Stock Photo; **p. 111** © Foto You/Adobe Stock Photo; **p. 112** *cr* © Aflo Co Ltd/Alamy Stock Photo; **p. 112** *br* © Subbotina Anna/Adobe Stock Photo; **p. 113** *tr* © Yakobchuk Olena/Adobe Stock Photo; **p. 114** *cr* © Fam Veldman/Adobe Stock Photo; **p. 116** *tr* © Akarakingdoms/Shutterstock.com; **p. 116** *cr* © Akarakingdoms/Shutterstock.com; **p. 116** *cr* © Akarakingdoms/Shutterstock.com; **p. 117** *tl* © Sean Gladwell/Adobe Stock Photo; **p. 117** *tr* © Maarten/Adobe Stock Photo; **p. 126** *br* © Nicknick Ko/Adobe Stock Photo; **p. 128** *cr* © Jason/Adobe Stock Photo; **p. 129** *tl, tc* © Eric Isselée/Adobe Stock Photo; **p. 129** *tr, b* © Sergiy 1607/Adobe Stock Photo; **p. 129** *cr* © A Dragan/Adobe Stock Photo; **p. 131** *cr* © Anna Velichkovsky/Adobe Stock Photo; **p. 131** © Blue Ring Media/Adobe Stock Photo; **p. 135** *tr* © Pamela D Mcadams/Adobe Stock Photo; **p. 136** *tr* © Riccardo Niels Mayer/Adobe Stock Photo; **p. 142** *cr* © Prochym/Adobe Stock Photo; **p. 143** © Alex Bush/Adobe Stock Photo; **p. 143** *cr* © Janaph/Adobe Stock Photo; **p. 143** *cr* © Anankkml/Adobe Stock Photo; **p. 143** *bl* © Shishiga/Adobe Stock Photo; **p. 149** *cc* © Eco View/Adobe Stock Photo; **p. 149** *cr*, **p. 155** *cr* © Okan/Adobe Stock Photo; **p. 151** *br* © Artush Foto/Adobe Stock Photo; **p. 154** *tr* © Mark Kostich/Adobe Stock Photo; **p. 154** *br* © Mike/Adobe Stock Photo; **p. 156** *tr* © Michael Drak/Adobe Stock Photo; **p. 159** *cl, p. 168 cr, p. 174 tr* © Aleksorel/Adobe Stock Photo; **p. 159** *cc* © Thannaree/Adobe Stock Photo; **p. 160** *cc* © New Africa/Adobe Stock Photo; **p. 161** *tr* © Scisetti Alfio/Adobe Stock Photo; **p. 162** *cr* © Richard Carey/Adobe Stock Photo; **p. 163** *bc* © Antonel/Adobe Stock Photo; **p. 164** *cr* © Whitcomberd/Adobe Stock Photo; **p. 165** *tl, tc* © Pixarno/Adobe Stock Photo; **p. 165** *tc* © Diveivanov/Adobe Stock Photo; **p. 165** *tc* © Andrey Kuzmin/Adobe Stock Photo; **p. 165** *tr* © Gmgadani/Adobe Stock Photo; **p. 165** *bl* © Rich Carey/Shutterstock.com; **p. 166** *cr, b* © Gresei/Adobe Stock Photo; **p. 167** *cr* © Raisondtre/Adobe Stock Photo; **p. 167** *br* © Auremar/Adobe Stock Photo; **p. 167** *br* © David Pereiras/Adobe Stock Photo; **p. 173** *cr* © Spyrakot/Adobe Stock Photo; **p. 173** *cc* © Coprid/Adobe Stock Photo; **p. 173** *br* © Aigarsr/Adobe Stock Photo; **p. 173** *bc* © Tina/Adobe Stock Photo; **p. 176** *cl* © Filirovska/Adobe Stock Photo; **p. 176** *cr* © Dimazel/Adobe Stock Photo; **p. 176** *bl* © Kajenna/Adobe Stock Photo; **p. 176** *br* © Roman Dekan/Adobe Stock Photo.

t = top, *b* = bottom, *l* = left, *r* = right, *c* = centre

Although every effort has been made to ensure that website addresses are correct at time of going to press, Hodder Education cannot be held responsible for the content of any website mentioned in this book. It is sometimes possible to find a relocated web page by typing in the address of the home page for a website in the URL window of your browser.

Hachette UK's policy is to use papers that are natural, renewable and recyclable products and made from wood grown in well-managed forests and other controlled sources. The logging and manufacturing processes are expected to conform to the environmental regulations of the country of origin.

Orders: please contact Hachette UK Distribution, Hely Hutchinson Centre, Milton Road, Didcot, Oxfordshire, OX11 7HH. Telephone: +44 (0)1235 827827. Email education@hachette.co.uk. Lines are open from 9 a.m. to 5 p.m., Monday to Saturday, with a 24-hour message answering service. You can also order through our website: www.hoddereducation.com

Cover illustration by Lisa Hunt

Illustrations by Steve Evans and Vian Oelofsen

Typeset in FS Albert 17/19 by IO Publishing CC

Produced by DZS Grafik, Printed in Slovenia

A catalogue record for this title is available from the British Library.

ISBN 9781398300200

MIX
Paper from responsible sources
FSC™ C104740
FSC
www.fsc.org

Contents

How to use this book

This tells you what the theme is about.

Learn new English skills with your teacher. Read the examples to help you.

Start: Read, write and talk about the text.

Go further and practise the skills.

Challenge yourself with these tasks.

Think about other topics you know.

Check the things you have learned in the unit.

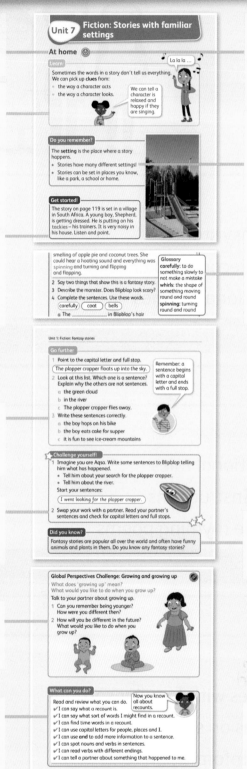

This theme has a digital resource for your teacher.

Remember a skill you have already learned.

Look here for the meaning of new words.

Read this interesting fact.

Find out how much you have learned at the end of the term by trying this quiz.

Aqsa's Adventures

Do you remember?

You need to hold your pencil correctly when you write.

- Remember to hold your pencil like this:

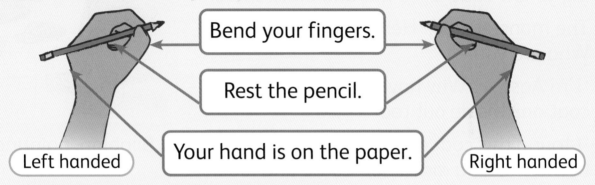

Bend your fingers.

Rest the pencil.

Your hand is on the paper.

Left handed

Right handed

- Sit with your back against the chair.
- Make sure your feet are flat on the ground.

Learn

Fantasy stories are about things that could not really happen in **real life**. They can have strange creatures, plants or talking animals. They can be set in strange and wonderful places that do not exist.

This unit is about *Aqsa's Adventures* by Rosemary Licciardi.

Have you read any fantasy stories? Which is your favourite?

Glossary
real life: the world we live in
fantasy: cannot happen in real life

Get started!

1 Listen and point.

Aqsa felt something was wrong, so she **carefully** opened the door. There, in front of her, stood a purple, furry monster with jingling bells in its hair, wearing her Mum's big yellow coat, a red hat and black socks.

The monster said, 'Hello. I am the Blipblop! Who are you?'

'I'm Aqsa … Why have you got my Mum's coat on? Inside out too!'

'I found this coat in my spinnermawinner,' said Blipblop, pointing to the washing machine. 'Come and look!'

Aqsa bent over to look in the washing machine, but she slipped on the end of the long yellow coat and fell in.

Suddenly, she was in a tunnel filled with bright orange **whirls** and smelling of apple pie and coconut trees. She could hear a hooting sound and everything was **spinning** and turning and flipping and flopping.

Glossary

carefully: to do something slowly to not make a mistake

whirls: the shape of something moving round and round

spinning: turning round and round

2 Say two things that show this is a fantasy story.

3 Describe the monster. Does Blipblop look scary?

4 Complete the sentences. Use these words.

(carefully) (coat) (bells)

a The _____ in Blipblop's hair make a jingling sound.

b Blipblop wears Aqsa's Mum's _____.

c Aqsa opened the door _____.

5 Practise writing each letter correctly. This will help you to write quickly and clearly.

Trace over the letters with your finger.

Make sure your feet are flat on the floor and that you are holding your pencil correctly.

a b c d e
f g h i j
k l m n o
p q r s t
u v w
x y z

Go further

Remember:
A **fantasy story** is one that is not set in the real world.

1 Listen to the story again. What funny things in the story would not happen in real life?

2 Point to the things you could find in a fantasy story, but not in a real-life story. Say why.

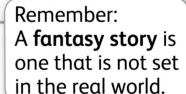

3 Read these words. Use the words to write some funny sentences.

(monkey) (camel) (trains) (books) (singing)

(purple) (coconut) (pizza)

a The _____ is eating the _____ trees.

b A _____ hat.

c A pair of _____ socks.

d A _____ coat.

4 a Find these words in the story. Read them aloud.

(trees) (out) (dream)

(coat) (hoots)

Look for these spelling pattern sounds:

(oo) (oa) (ee) (ou)

b Think of a rhyming word for each word. Write the new words.

⭐ Challenge yourself!

1 Listen to the story *Aqsa's Adventures* again.

2 a Create or draw Blipblop the monster.

b What do you think Aqsa will say when she gets to the end of the tunnel? Write the words.

3 Imagine the creatures and plants that Aqsa will find at the end of the tunnel.

a Draw them next to Blipblop.

b Name each creature and plant.

Art

Create a collage of Blipblop. Make sure you include his hat, coat and socks.

Write labels to describe his clothes.

1 A _____ hat

2 A _____ coat

3 _____ socks

Strange places – familiar words

Do you remember?

Can you read these words? You can't blend the sounds to read them. You just have to learn them!

(was) (his) (my) (asked)

(said) (the) (called) (off)

For **was** we say (woz), for **his** we say (hiz), for **said** we say (sed).

Get started!

1 Listen and point. Can you spot any of the words above?

'Welcome Aqsa! You're in my country, Blipblopia,' said Blipblop.

'It looks lovely here!' said Aqsa. 'What is that called?' she asked, pointing to a blue and green seashell on a plate.

'That is a plopper cropper and they are **delicious** to eat,' said Blipblop, and they watched as it clapped its shells and floated off.

'You must catch it,' he said and **whistled**. A green cloud **zoomed** down from the sky and Aqsa jumped into it. It felt **fluffy**.

'Wow!' said Aqsa.

Glossary

delicious: tastes very good

whistled: making a noise by blowing through the lips and teeth

zoomed: moved very quickly

fluffy: something that is soft and light

9

2 Which word tells you that Aqsa is happy to jump into the cloud? Write the word.

said   Wow!   floated

3 Read and write the words:

my   said   called   asked   off   the

Make a tick next to each word when you find it in the story.

4 Choose a word from above to complete these sentences.

Say the words aloud. Listen to the different sounds.

a The seashell is

_____

a plopper cropper.

b The plopper cropper floated _____.

c Blipblop _____ Aqsa must catch the plopper cropper.

5 Look at the picture of Aqsa and Blipblop. Describe the picture to your partner.

Go further

1 Read these words. Practise spelling them.

(my) (said) (called) (asked) (off) (the)

> **Look** – say the word.
> **Cover** – hide the word.
> **Write** – write the word.
> **Check** – check your spelling.

2 Read the words below. Look for each word in the story on pages 6 and 9. Write the word when you find it.

(trees) (coat) (hat) (socks) (cloud) (fluffy)

3 You are Aqsa and Blipblop. Imagine that you are eating a meal in Blipblopia. What will you order to eat? Talk to your partner about your ideas. Write a menu with your partner.

Challenge yourself!

1 Talk about the picture on page 10 with a partner.

2 Write a sentence about the picture, for example:

> The tree is yellow and pink.

Global Perspectives Challenge: Fun with fruit!

Does fruit taste sweet or sour?

1 Taste some fruits. Sort them into sweet or sour. Choose a way to show your results.

2 Create a funny face with the fruits. Make up a silly story about your fruit face!

Sentences

Do you remember?

A **sentence** has a **capital letter** at the beginning and a **full stop** at the end.

(T)he boy has an egg for breakfast(.)

| capital letter | full stop |

Learn

Practise writing each capital letter correctly.

A B C D E
F G H I J
K L M N O
P Q R S T
U V W
X Y Z

Trace over the letters with your finger.

Get started!

1 Listen and point. Aqsa and Blipblop are looking for the plopper cropper.

Aqsa flew over ice-cream mountains. She looked under rocks, up tall trees and in dark caves.

Suddenly, she **noticed** a group of plopper croppers beside a lemonade river. The green cloud slowed down. Aqsa took off her **slippers** with bells and **tiptoed** towards the river.

Glossary
noticed: spotted
slippers: warm shoes to wear in a house
tiptoed: walked very quietly on your toes

2 Read the story text with your teacher. Pause at the end of each sentence.

3 Count the number of sentences in the text. Write the number.

4 Why did Aqsa take off her slippers with bells? Tell your partner.

5 Aqsa spotted the cloud of plopper croppers. Which word means **noticed**? Write the word.

(fell) (made) (saw)

6 Find these words in the story text on page 12.

(in) (up) (under) (over)

7 Imagine Aqsa is still looking for the plopper cropper. Write your own sentence for each word in question 6. For example:

Aqsa looked **under** a chair.   She looked **up** the stairs.

Go further

1 Point to the capital letter and full stop.

> The plopper cropper floats up into the sky.

Remember: a sentence begins with a capital letter and ends with a full stop.

2 Look at this list. Which one is a sentence? Explain why the others are not sentences.

   a the green cloud

   b in the river

   c The plopper cropper flies away.

3 Write these sentences correctly.

   a the boy hops on his bike

   b the boy eats cake for supper

   c it is fun to see ice-cream mountains

⭐ Challenge yourself!

1 Imagine you are Aqsa. Write some sentences to Blipblop telling him what has happened.

- Tell him about your search for the plopper cropper.
- Tell him about the river.

Start your sentences:

> I went looking for the plopper cropper.

2 Swap your work with a partner. Read your partner's sentences and check for capital letters and full stops.

Did you know?

Fantasy stories are popular all over the world and often have funny animals and plants in them. Do you know any fantasy stories?

Aqsa

Characters are the people or animals that you meet in the story. In *Aqsa's Adventures*, the characters are:

Aqsa

the plopper cropper

Blipblop

the mother plopper cropper

The **main character** is the most important character.

Aqsa is the **main character**.

15

Get started!

1 Listen and point.

When Aqsa arrived at the river, the plopper croppers started flying around her. The lemonade river started to whirl. A very big plopper cropper, with large yellow eyes that were looking right at Aqsa, came out of the water. Aqsa ran as fast as she could.

'Help! It's the mother plopper cropper!' she cried.

2 Why does Aqsa run away from the lemonade river? Tell your partner.

3 How does Aqsa feel as she tiptoes towards the river? Read these words. Choose one.

(happy)　(nervous)　(angry)　(interested)

4 How does Aqsa feel when she runs away from the river? Read these words. Choose one.

(sleepy)　(scared)　(happy)　(interested)

5 What does each character do? Write the character's name for each sentence.

(Aqsa)　(Blipblop)　(Plopper croppers)　(Mother plopper cropper)

a _____ flies on a green cloud.

b _____ comes out of the lemonade river.

c _____ swim in the lemonade river.

d _____ wears funny clothes.

Go further

1 Describe the mother plopper cropper to your partner. Write a sentence about her.

2 Look at the little plopper croppers. How do they feel? Are they happy that their mother is scaring Aqsa? What do you think they are saying? Tell your partner.

3 What do you think the mother plopper cropper will do next? Tell your partner.

Challenge yourself!

1 Copy and complete the sentences. Use these words:

(scared) (nervous) (excited) (surprised)

a When the plopper cropper flies away, Aqsa feels _____.

b When Aqsa looks for the plopper cropper, she _____.

c When Aqsa tiptoes towards the river, she feels _____.

d When Aqsa sees the mother plopper cropper, she feels

_____.

2 Look at these three characters:

a What do you think they are like?

b Who do you think should be the main character?

c Make up the start of a story about the characters.

17

Words, words, words

Do you remember?

When you see a new word that looks difficult to read:

- Look at each letter. Is it making a sound on its own, or is it working with another letter?
- Look for two or three letters making one sound, for example:

(sh) (ou) (th) (qu) (bb) (ere)

- Look for letters that need to be blended together, for example:

(nt) (st) (dr) (sw)

Practise reading these words from the story on page 19:

- **slipper** (s-l-i-p-er)
- **clapping** (c-l-a-p-i-ng)
- **jingled** (j-i-ng-l-ed).

Sometimes the pictures in a story will give you a clue.

Ask your teacher to help you read the parts you do not know.

Learn

Some words are great to use when describing a chase. Read these words:

(around) (along) (up) (over)

Read and find the words in the story on the next page.

Get started!

1 Listen and point.

> The mother plopper cropper chased Aqsa along the lemonade river, clapping her shells angrily at her. The bells on Aqsa's slippers jingled loudly as she ran. The mother plopper cropper chased her over the ice-cream mountains, up the tall trees and around the caves.
>
> 'Clap, clap, clap!' The mother plopper cropper was getting closer and closer! Then, suddenly, Aqsa was flying high in the sky on the green cloud and the clapping sound was becoming quieter and quieter.

2 Read the story with your teacher. Talk about which words are difficult to read.

3 How does Aqsa escape?

4 Where did the mother plopper cropper chase Aqsa? Complete the sentences. Use these words.

(around)   (along)   (over)   (up)

> Blend the sounds to read the words.

  a She chased her _____ the lemonade river.

  b She chased her _____ the ice-cream mountains.

  c She chased her _____ the tall trees.

  d She chased her _____ the caves.

5 Why do you think the mother plopper cropper chased Aqsa? How did the mother plopper cropper feel? How did Aqsa feel?

Go further

1 Read and find these words in the story on page 19.

> clapping   slipper

Make up a sentence using each word and tell your partner.

2 Start a *Spelling log*. Write your favourite words from this story, such as:

> clapping   slipper   jingling

3 Role-play what happened in the story. You could use one of these sentences:

- A green cloud saved me today.

- A scary mother plopper cropper chased me today.

4 Write some sentences to show what happened to your character. Try to use one of your favourite words from the story.

> Try to spell the words yourself, but ask for help if you are unsure.

⭐ Challenge yourself!

Where would you like the mother plopper cropper to chase Aqsa? Copy and complete these sentences. Make up funny places for the chase.

1 The mother plopper cropper chased the Aqsa **over** the _____ and **along** the _____.

2 She chased her **around** the _____ and **up** the _____.

Beginning, middle and end

Learn

We can use the words (**beginning**), (**middle**) and (**end**) to talk about a story.

- *Beginning*: We meet the character. An adventure starts.
- *Middle*: The main part of the story.
- *End*: The story finishes.

Look at this story:

Beginning: *A girl goes to stay with her granny.*

Middle: *She can't find her toy cat. She searches everywhere in Granny's house.*

End: *She finds her toy cat at home on her bed.*

Get started!

1 The clapping noise of the mother plopper cropper is getting quieter and quieter.

The green cloud was so soft and Aqsa was so sleepy after running so far for so long that she closed her eyes. She pulled the soft cloud over herself and fell asleep.

Hours and hours later, Aqsa woke up. Was it a dream, she wondered?

2 Tell your partner what happens at the end of the story.

3 Read the sentences and decide with a partner if they happen at the **beginning**, **middle** or **end** of the story.

Aqsa falls into the washing machine.

The mother plopper cropper chases Aqsa.

Aqsa chases the plopper cropper.

Aqsa goes to sleep.

The green cloud saves Aqsa.

Aqsa wakes up.

Beginning	Middle	End

Go further

1 Write one more sentence in each section from *Get started!* question 3.

2 Look at the picture of Aqsa's bedroom. Talk about the picture with your partner. Find characters from the story in the picture.

   a Can you see the picture of a plopper cropper?

   b Can you see Blipblop?

   c Can you see the green cloud mobile?

3 You are now going to tell the beginning, middle and end of *Aqsa's Adventures*. Look at these pictures. Tell your partner what is happening in each picture. Can you use some of the interesting words from the book?

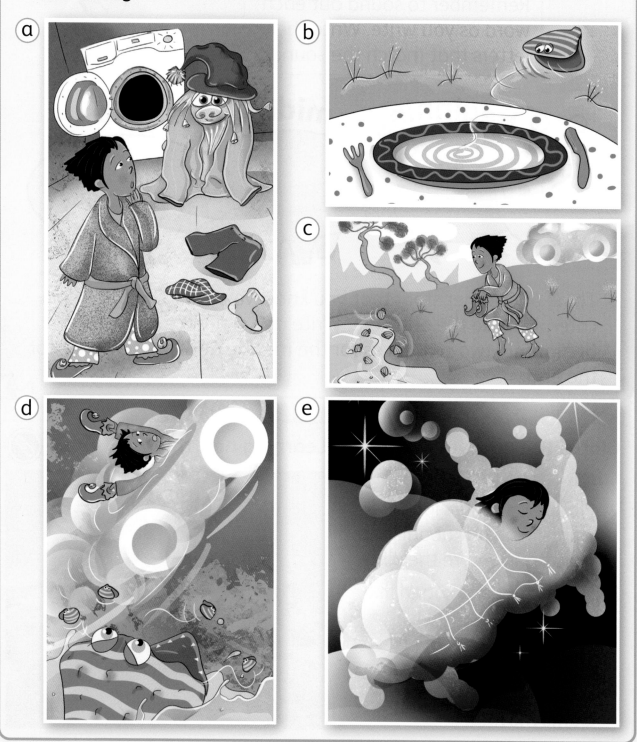

Challenge yourself!

1 Write a caption for each picture of your story from *Go further* question 3.

Remember to sound out each word as you write. Write the letters that match the sounds.

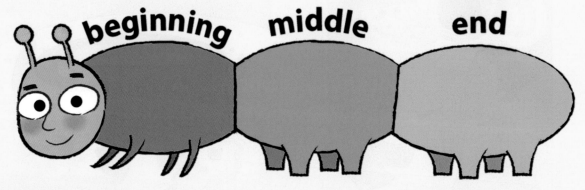

beginning   **middle**   **end**

2 Think of another story that you know very well. Draw a story caterpillar like the one here. Write one sentence for the **beginning**, two sentences for the **middle** and one sentence for the **end**.

Global Perspectives Challenge: Learning new things

Learning a new skill

1 Plopper croppers look like clams. Find out about clams and where they live.

2 What do clams sound like when they move? Use musical instruments to create a simple or rhythm tune that sounds like clams moving.

My fantasy story

Do you remember?

Stories have a **beginning**, a **middle** and an **end**. We can use this to plan out a new fantasy story.

beginning

Wim looks for her friend Wam.

middle

Wim sees Wam's tail. She pulls the tail. It is a big monster. The monster chases Wim.

end

Wam saves Wim. They fly to the top of a tree.

What absurd place can you make up? What strange creatures live there?

Learn

We add **s** or **es** to some **nouns** to show there is **more than one** of them.

A **noun** is an object or thing. For example, **dragon**, **box** and **monster**.

one monster

two monster**s**

one box

two box**es**

Get started!

1 Find and copy all the nouns that end in **s**.

(cloud) (trees) (monsters) (mountains) (coat)

(flowers) (river) (cave) (scarf) (slippers)

2 Add **s** to these nouns. Write the words.

(dream) (pencil) (machine) (bed) (eye)

Can you spot these spelling patterns?

(ee) (ow) (ar) (ea)

3 Look at this story.

beginning

beginning

middle

middle

end

Use phonics to write the names. Ask for help if you need it.

Make up a name for each character.
Write the names.

4 Practise using the pictures to tell a story.

a Here are some funny names to use in your story.

one glump	two glumps
one bish	two bishes
one wox	two woxes

b Can you read the made-up nouns in the table on page 26? Can you hear the **s** or **es** ending?

c Draw three circles and write the words you will use to tell your story.

Beginning
has these words:

friend
find
sad
hunt

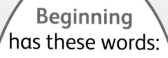

Middle
has these words:

tail
pull
monster
run
scared

End
has these words:

friend
tree
happy

Go further

1 Choose one of these story starters:

- Once upon a time …

- There once was …

- One sunny day …

b Write a sentence to go with each picture. Sound out each word carefully. Use the letters you know for each sound.

c Read your story aloud. Tell a partner which part you are most pleased with: the **beginning**, **middle** or **end**.

Can you say how your character feels?

Remember to use a capital letter at the start and a full stop at the end of the sentence.

Challenge yourself!

1 Make up your own story for the creatures on page 26.

a Plan what will happen in the beginning, middle and end. Draw a chart of a story caterpillar to help you plan.

b Tell your story to a partner before you write it down. You could use these ideas:

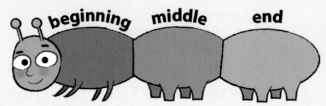

- *The friend is in trouble and needs to be rescued.*
- *The friend is playing in a monster's garden.*
- *The friend has made a flying machine.*

Can you use some of these words to show what is happening? **along**, **around**, **up**, **over**

What can you do?

Read and review what you can do.

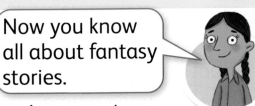

Now you know all about fantasy stories.

✔ I can hold my pencil correctly.

✔ I can say what a fantasy story is.

✔ I can use a capital letter and a full stop in my sentences.

✔ I can tell a friend who the main characters are in a story.

✔ I can blend sounds to try and read new words.

✔ I can use these words in my writing: **along**, **around**, **up**, **over**.

✔ I can spot nouns that end in **s** or **es** to show there is more than one.

✔ I can talk about what is happening in the beginning, middle and end of a story.

✔ I can plan and write a new story with a beginning, middle and end.

✔ I can tell a friend a story I know.

Postcards

Do you remember?

We use a capital letter for:

- the first word in a sentence
- the word **I**
- the names of people
- the names of places.

Yesterday, I went swimming.

We use a capital letter for the word **I**.

We moved to Lagos.

We use a capital letter for **L**agos because it is a place.

We use a capital letter for **I** and for **names** even if they are in the middle of a sentence.

Ben visited the city of Abuja.

We use a capital letter for **B**en because it is a name and **A**buja because it is a place.

Learn

A **recount** is the retelling of something that happened to you or to someone else. A recount:

- is about something that happened in the past
- uses time words such as *first*, *then* and *next*
- is about one person or a group of people.

Get started!

1 Ravi has gone to Cape Town in South Africa on holiday. Listen and point to this postcard from Ravi to her friend.

Dear Diya

We are in Cape Town.
On Tuesday, I snorkelled
with seals. One seal nudged
me! Yesterday, we visited
Boulders Beach with our
friends Max and April.
There were penguins on the
beach! They waddled around
and looked so funny.

From Ravi

Diya Banerjee

4654 Besant Road

Chennai

Tamil Nadu 600078

India

2 Where has Ravi gone on holiday?

3 Write two things that Ravi has done on holiday.

4 Point to the capital letters. Tell your partner why they are used.

5 Pretend you are Ravi and your partner is Diya. Have a pretend telephone conversation about the holiday. Add extra things you have done.

6 Find and point to these words: (On Tuesday) (Yesterday)

7 What did you do yesterday?
Write a sentence. Start your sentence:

Yesterday, I _____
_____.

Glossary
Cape Town: a big city in South Africa
Chennai: a big city in India

Go further

Pretend that you are on holiday in Cape Town.

1 Which of these activities did you do? Tell your partner.
2 Write a postcard to a friend about your activity.
3 Read your writing. Check that you have used a capital letter for:
   - the start of sentences
   - names of places
   - names of people
   - the pronoun **I**.

played on Clifton beach

went on a scooter trip

shopped in the market

went in a cable car up Table Mountain

Challenge yourself!

Write a postcard to a child in another country. Tell them what you have done this week.

- Include words about time such as *Yesterday* or *On the weekend*.
- Write about two different things you have done (one can be going to school).
- Write the activities in the order you did them.

Global Perspectives Challenge: Growing and growing up

What is it like growing up in a different country?

Find out more about growing up in Cape Town, South Africa.

1 How is it different to where you live?
2 How is it the same?

If you live in South Africa, then choose another country.

Dear Diary

Do you remember?

We can use the word **and** to add information.

- *I visited Auntie Flo **and** Uncle Baz.*
- *We ate chicken **and** rice.*

We can also use **and** to join together two parts of a sentence.

- *We visited Auntie Flo **and** we saw the new baby.*

The word **and** is a joining word.

- *We played games **and** we watched television.*

Learn

A **recount** can be:

- a diary
- a letter or a postcard
- a report of a visit
- a newspaper report of something that happened.

Do you like reading recounts?

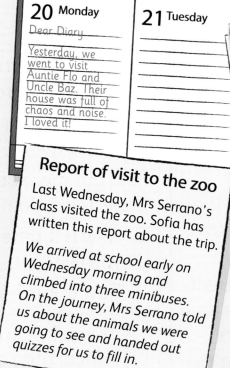

APRIL 2020

20 Monday
Dear Diary

Yesterday, we went to visit Auntie Flo and Uncle Baz. Their house was full of chaos and noise. I loved it!

21 Tuesday

Dear Diya
We are in Cape Town.
On Tuesday, I snorkelled with seals. One seal nudged me! Yesterday, we visited Boulders Beach with our friends Max and April. There were penguins on the beach! They waddled around and looked so funny.

From Ravi

Diya Banerjee

4654 Besant Road

Chennai

Tamil Nadu 600078

India

Report of visit to the zoo

Last Wednesday, Mrs Serrano's class visited the zoo. Sofia has written this report about the trip.

We arrived at school early on Wednesday morning and climbed into three minibuses. On the journey, Mrs Serrano told us about the animals we were going to see and handed out quizzes for us to fill in.

CITY PRESS
STATE VISIT TO ZOO

Last Monday, the President visited City Zoo. The President was visiting the area for the first time.

The President was shown the zoo's newest resident – a baby giraffe.

Get started!

1 Faith has visited her relatives. Listen and point to the diary entry of the day. Can you find the word **and**?

24 April

Dear Diary

Yesterday, we went to visit Auntie Flo and Uncle Baz. I loved it! I had a great time with my cousins, Gloria and Grace. We chatted and laughed as we played together. My brother ran around the yard and chased the chickens. Auntie Flo showed us where to find eggs and let us milk the goat.

At night, I slept in Gloria and Grace's room. I could hear Mummy and Auntie chatting, Uncle Baz singing and the goat **bleating**.

2 Read the text aloud with your teacher. Pause at the full stops.

3 Point to the capital letters. Say why each has been used.

4 What sounds can Faith hear? Tell your partner. Use **and** in your sentence.

5 Write what sounds you can hear in your house at night. Use **and** in your sentence.

6 Remember a time when you visited relatives. Write about the visit as a diary entry. Start your diary like this:

Dear Diary
Yesterday, I visited _____.
I _____
_____.

Remember to use a capital letter for a name.

Glossary
bleating: the noise a goat makes

Go further

1 Faith goes shopping to buy presents. Read the labels in the picture.

2 Choose two presents for each person. Copy and complete the sentences. Remember to use **and**.

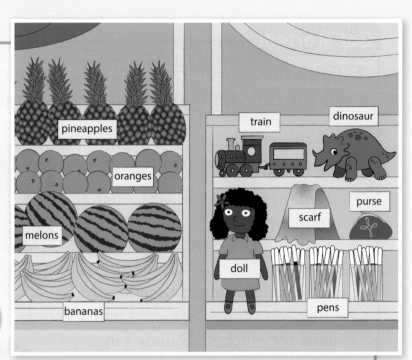

a For Tashie, I bought _____.

b For Obi, I bought _____.

c For Granny, I bought _____.

3 What did Faith buy for herself? Choose two things. Write a sentence.

Challenge yourself!

1 Imagine that Faith has come to visit your family.

a Who lives in your house? What is your house like?

b What games would you play?

c Where would you take Faith?

Remember to write things that have happened.

2 Write Faith's diary entry for the day. Start the diary like this:

Dear Diary

Today, I visited _____.

A trip to the zoo

A **noun** is a person, place or thing.

The panda chews the bamboo.

nouns

A **verb** is a doing word.

The monkeys are chattering.

The lions roared.

The hippo sleeps.

verbs

Verbs can end in **s**, **ing** and **ed**.

Do you remember?

We can add **s** or **es** to a noun to show there is **more than one**.

one shark

two sharks

one fox

two fox**es**

Can you hear the **es** end in fox**es**?

Get started!

1 Listen and read this report about a class trip from a school's newsletter. Try to spot nouns and verbs as you read.

Springfield School News

17 May Week 20

Last Wednesday, Mrs Serrano's class visited the zoo. Sofia wrote this report about the trip:

On Wednesday, three minibuses took us to the zoo.

When we arrived, we left our lunch boxes in the canteen. Then we rushed to see the penguins being fed. How they shuffled on land and zipped and whizzed under water!

After that, we watched the monkeys monkeying around and the flying foxes leaping from tree to tree. Next, we went to the reptile house. The snakes gave me the creeps, but I loved the tortoises and the chameleons. After the reptile house, it was time for lunch.

After lunch we went to the aquarium and saw fish, sharks and a very shy octopus.

Finally, it was time to get back on the minibuses. Most of us slept all the way back to school.

Glossary

minibuses: small buses
canteen: dining hall
shuffled: walked without picking up their feet
whizzed: moved fast
monkeying around: fooling around
reptile: an animal with scaly skin like a lizard, a snake or a crocodile
the creeps: a scary feeling

2 Tell your partner:

   a When did the trip take place?

   b Who went on the trip?

   c Read these words. Find them in the report.

      (After that) (Next) (Finally)

   d What animals did the children see?

3 Write this sentence.

   (We watched the monkey in the tree.)

   a Circle the verb.

   b Underline two nouns.

4 Read these words. Find and copy the noun in each of these lines:

   a (zebra)   (eats)   (drinks)

   b (saw)   (hippo)   (sleeping)

   c (sat)   (jumped)   (octopus)

Speak clearly so your partner can hear you.

Remember: nouns are people, places or things.

5 Copy this table. Sort the words into those ending in **s** and those ending in **es**. The first two have been done for you.

(quizzes) (groups) (boxes) (foxes) (sharks) (chameleons)

Ending es	Ending s
buses	*monkeys*

Go further

1 Copy and complete each line using **s** or **es**.

Read the words aloud. Can you hear the **s** or **es** ending?

  a two lunch box_____   b two quiz_____

  c three shark_____   d four fox_____

  e five penguin_____

2 a Read these sentences.
     Point to the nouns and verbs.

The tiger drinks the water.

The owl looked at the boy.

The red panda is sitting in the tree.

  b Pretend you have been to the zoo and seen these animals.
     Write a recount. Start your report:

Last week I went to the zoo. I saw _____.

Challenge yourself!

What is your favourite animal?

1 Draw a picture of your animal.

2 Write some sentences about how your animal looks.

3 Write what your animal does.

Science

1 Find out where your favourite animal lives in the wild.

  a Does it live in a hot place or a cold place?

  b What does it like to eat? Find out different facts about your favourite animal.

2 Tell the class or a small group all about your animal.

My first day of school

Do you remember?

Have you read other recounts at school or home?

A **recount**:

- tells about something that happened in the past
- uses words such as *first*, *then*, *next* and *finally*
- tells the events in the order they happened
- is about something that happened to a person.

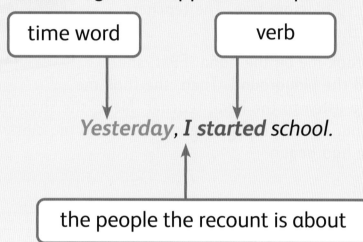

| time word | verb |

Yesterday, I started school.

the people the recount is about

Learn

We use **past tense verbs** when we write recounts.
This shows that an action happened in the past.
These verbs tell us about things that have already happened:

walked   helped   mended

ended   jumped   greeted

washed   showed

Listen to the **ed** at the end of the word. Does it sound like **d**, **t** or **ed**?

Get started!

1 Listen and read. Try to spot verbs ending in **ed**.

Dear Granny

Yesterday I started school. Daddy gave me a new backpack with pencils and paper. Mummy filled a box with charaben (cute characters made from rice and other foods) for my lunch.

We walked to school. Daddy took a photo of me under the cherry blossom tree. The teachers greeted us at the gate.

An older girl took me by the hand. First, she led me around the playground. Then, she took me into the hall to listen to the head teacher. Next, she showed me where to put my shoes. Finally, she walked me to my classroom. My school life had begun.

Love from Min

2 Point to these words in the recount.

(First) (Then) (Next) (Finally)

These **time words** show you the order in which the events happened.

3 Find and copy all the verbs in the letter that end in **ed**. Read the words.

Does the **ed** sound like **d**, **t** or **ed**?

4 a Tell your partner about your first day of school.

   b Write about it. Try to use some of these words:

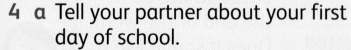

(At last)   (Next)   (First)   (and)

Go further

1   Pretend you are the girl remembering her first day at school. Write a caption for each picture. Use these sentence starters.

> Remember: write as if you are remembering things that happened in the past.

*   First, I arrived _____.
*   Then, I chatted to _____.
*   Next, we looked _____.

Here are useful words that you can use:

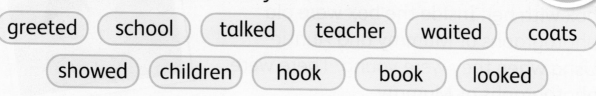

(greeted)   (school)   (talked)   (teacher)   (waited)   (coats)

(showed)   (children)   (hook)   (book)   (looked)

2   Read your writing. Check that you have used a capital letter and a full stop for each caption. Have you used a capital letter for **I**?

Challenge yourself!

What did you do at school yesterday? Write a recount. Use time words to show the order of the day.

Did you know?

Children start school at different ages around the world.
*   In France, children start school at 3.
*   In England, children start school at 4 and in Nigeria, they start at 5.
*   In Malaysia children start school at 7.

Growing up

Learn

Verbs can end in **s**, **ed** and **ing**.

- *Kai sometimes **walks** to school with Ben.*
- *Kai is **walking** home now.*
- *Kai **walked** to school this morning.*

Verbs that end in **ed** show that the event took place in the past.

Get started!

1   Listen and point to this recount. Look out for verbs ending in **ing** and verbs ending in **ed**.

Last time Granny visited she brought a box with her. Inside the box were old photographs of Mummy and Auntie Usha when they were young. There were photographs of Mummy crawling and photographs of Mummy cuddling baby Auntie Usha. I could see Mummy growing up!

Mummy first sat up when she was five months old.

Mummy walked on her first birthday.

2 Find and copy two verbs that end in **ing**.
  Find and copy two verbs that end in **ed**.

3 Tell your partner how you know that this is a recount.

4 How have you changed over the last few years?
  - What have you learned to do?
  - Write about how you have grown.

Copy and complete these sentences:

Speak clearly so that your partner can hear you.

Growing up

When I was a baby, I learned _____.

When I was one, I _____.

When I was two, I _____.

When I was three, I _____.

When I was four, _____.

Now I am _____.

5 Draw a picture of yourself to go with your recount.

Do you remember?

We use a **capital letter** to start a sentence and at the start of a person's name. Practise writing each capital letter correctly.

Trace over the letters with your finger.

A B C D E
F G H I J
K L M N O
P Q R S T
U V W
X Y Z

Go further

1   You are growing up all the time! Think of a new skill you have learned to do in the last year. Here are some ideas:

- ride a bike
- play a game
- write your name
- read a book

- skip with a rope
- tie a bow
- walk to school.

2   Do you remember how you learned to do the new skill? Tell your partner how you got better. Use these time words:

(First)   (Then)   (Now)

3   Write a recount about how you learned your new skill, for example:

- **First**, I traced over my name.
- **Then**, I copied my name.
- **Now** I, can write my name without help.

Challenge yourself!

Remember a day when you did something brave, such as:

- *went on a sleepover*
- *climbed high on the climbing frame*
- *tried to swim without your arm bands*
- *read a story aloud in class.*

Write a **recount** to show what happened.

- Start the first sentence like this:

(When I was _____.)

- Start the last sentence like this:

(Now I know _____.)

Global Perspectives Challenge: Growing and growing up

What does 'growing up' mean?
What would you like to do when you grow up?

Talk to your partner about growing up.

1 Can you remember being younger?
   How were you different then?

2 How will you be different in the future?
   What would you like to do when you
   grow up?

What can you do?

Read and review what you can do.

✔ I can say what a recount is.

✔ I can say what sort of words
   I might find in a recount.

✔ I can find time words in a recount.

✔ I can use capital letters for people, places and **I**.

✔ I can use **and** to add more information to a sentence.

✔ I can spot nouns and verbs in sentences.

✔ I can read verbs with different endings.

✔ I can tell a partner about something that happened to me.

Now you know all about recounts.

Unit 3 Poetry: Traditional rhymes

Counting in the Caribbean

Do you remember?

We can spell out numbers to ten.

1	2	3	4	5
one	two	three	four	five
6	7	8	9	10
six	seven	eight	nine	ten

Read each number. Which one is the hardest to spell?

Get started!

1 Listen and point to the rhyme from the Caribbean on page 47. Clap along with the beat of the rhyme like this:

Mosquito one, Mosquito two, Mosquito jump in the <u>callaloo</u>.

Can you hear the rhythm of the rhyme as you say it?

2 **a** Find these phrases:

jump in the callaloo   fly out the old man door

break up the old man bricks   open the old man gate

tickle the old man hen

b Tell your partner what the mosquito is doing in each phrase.

46

Mosquito One

Mosquito one,
Mosquito two,
Mosquito jump in the **callaloo**.
Mosquito three,
Mosquito four,
Mosquito fly out the old man door.
Mosquito five,
Mosquito six,
Mosquito break up the old man bricks.
Mosquito seven,
Mosquito eight,
Mosquito open the old man gate.
Mosquito nine,
Mosquito ten,
Mosquito tickle the old man hen.

Traditional Caribbean rhyme

Glossary

mosquito: a small biting insect

callaloo: a hot dish made with green vegetables

Words that **rhyme** end with the same sound but are not always spelled the same. For example: *four* and *door*.

3 Find and copy the verb in each long line in the rhyme. The first one is **jump**.

Most verbs are 'doing' words: **jump**, **open** and **fly** are all **verbs**.

4 Count and write the missing number word.

a _____ bugs jumping	
b _____ ants lifting	
c _____ legs dancing	

Go further

Use the rhythm of the rhyme to make it fun to listen to.

1 With your partner, make up an action for each long line in the rhyme.

2 Learn the rhyme on page 47 off by heart and say it while doing your actions.

3 Perform the rhyme to the rest of the class.

4 Copy the number and write the rhyming word from the rhyme.

   a two _____

   b four _____

   c six _____

   d eight _____

   e ten _____

Circle the pair of words that have the same spelling pattern.

Challenge yourself!

1 Copy and finish this new mosquito rhyme. Use these ideas:

(tasty stew)   (sticky glue)   (bathroom floor)   (local store)

(pile of sticks)   (cookie mix)   (china plate)   (garden gate)

(the silly men)   (my Uncle Ben)

Mosquito one,
Mosquito two,
Mosquito swim in the _____.
Mosquito three,
Mosquito four,
Mosquito creep along the _____.
Mosquito five,
Mosquito six,
Mosquito land on the _____.
Mosquito seven,
Mosquito eight,
Mosquito sit on the _____.
Mosquito nine,
Mosquito ten,
Mosquito bite _____.

Geography

1 Find the Caribbean region on a map.

2 What is the weather like in the Caribbean? Find out and then tell the class.

An English alphabet

a b c d e
f g h i j
k l m n o
p q r s t
u v w
x y z

Do you remember?

Say and write each letter. Check that your feet are flat on the floor. Check that you are holding your pencil correctly.

Trace over the letters with your finger.

Get started!

1 Say and clap this alphabet rhyme from England.

a, b, c, d,

e, f, g,

h, i, j, k,

l, m, n, o, p,

q, r, s,

t, u, v,

w, x,

y and z.

2 There is another alphabet rhyme on page 51. Listen and point. Then say the rhyme aloud and clap the beat.

Alphabet chant

A is for auntie, hugging me tight

B is for bats, flying at night

C is for cats and cheese and caves

D is for Dad and digging and Dave

E is for eggs, all yellow and white

F is for fishy fish 'n fighty fights

G is for **goo 'n gunk** 'n **gobbledeegook**

H is for hope, happiness, hooks

I is for **icky** ink and **inky** ice

J is jumping for joy and jellies ... nice!

K is my friend Kuka, kites and karate

L is licking lollies and loving **lattes**

M is for monkey, marshmallow and **mews**

N is for **napkin**, notes and news

O is for over, **ostrich** and **omelette**

And P is for Pupa, my **precious**, perfect pet

Q is for quite quiet queens queuing in a queue

R is my favourite for ruby, red rose and **roux**

S is for shoes, sausages sizzling in pans

T is for things and tails and **tans**

U starts unicorns, up and under the moon

V starts vans, **vacation** and **vroom**

W is for Winston, whistling and wiggy woo

X is hard ... can you think of one or two?

Y is **yummy** and **yucky** and **yak** and you

Z is for **Zumba**, zoom and zoo!

By Rosemary Licciardi

Glossary

goo 'n gunk: dirty and sticky things

gobbledeegook: nonsense

icky: not very nice

inky: covered in ink

lattes: a hot drink

mews: a house

napkin: cloth or paper used to protect your clothes when eating

ostrich: a bird

omelette: eggs, beaten and cooked

precious: something that means a lot to you

roux: a sauce

tans: what happens to your skin when you spend time in the sun

vacation: a holiday

vroom: the sound a vehicle makes

yummy: this is good to eat

yucky: this is not good to eat

yak: an animal

Zumba: an exercise class

3 Find and copy a word or letter in the rhyme that rhymes with:

(bats) (cooks) (waves) (vans) (set)

Go further

1 Read these words. Find and write pairs of words that rhyme.

| arrow | bog | barrow | clock |

| dock | East | fog | feast |

2 Now write your own poem! Choose a word to complete each line. Can you make some lines rhyme?

a is for _____ (acorn, arrow, ant)

b is for _____ (barrow, bee, bump, bog)

c is for _____ (clock, carrot)

d is for _____ (dock, dog, drum)

e is for _____ (elephant, eagle, East)

f is for _____ (fog, frog, farm, feast)

Challenge yourself!

1 Learn your own poem off by heart.

2 Draw a picture for each noun and then perform your poem to the class. Hold up your pictures as you perform your poem.

Remember that a **noun** is an object, an animal, a thing or a person.

Did you know?

There are 26 letters in the English alphabet. This sentence uses every letter in the alphabet!

The quick brown fox jumps over the lazy dog.

An animal rhyme from Australia

Do you remember?

Some letters work together to make one sound.
For example:

(**sh**)   (**ch**)   (**ng**)   (**ck**)   (**tch**)

ship   chip   sing   pick   patch

fish   watch

Some letters are often found together.

beach

We must blend the letters together:

(**bl**) (**nk**) (**pl**) (**cr**) (**br**) (**ld**) (**sl**) (**pr**) (**squ**)

blink   sink   plank   creek   bring   fold   slip   prong   squid

Get started!

> Look for letters that blend together.

1 Read these letters. Do they make one, two or three sounds?

(cr) (fl) (pr) (squ) (str) (scr)

2 Match the words with the same opening letters. Write the words as pairs.

(squawk)   (flap)   (shout)   (squeak)

(shiver)   (chatter)   (chitter)   (flip)

3 Listen and point as your teacher reads this rhyme from Australia. Can you find these pairs of letters in any word?

 ck   tch   ch   qu   th

Chooks in the
chook yard
    dust flick
    scritch scratch
    pick peck
    chook chat

Chooks on the
pen roof
    air stare
    primp preen
    strut *smart*
    chook squawk

Chooks on the
roosting rail
    claw grab
    bottom **squat**
    feather fluff
    chook **croon**

You chooks
in the chook yard
on the roosting rail
and on the pen roof
get into the nesting boxes
now
and
LAY SOME EGGS!

By Janeen Brian

4 Read the rhyme with a partner. What are the chickens doing? List the verbs that tell you.

Go further

1 Learn the first **verse** with a partner. Say the rhyme together.

2 Look at this picture. Write a new verse about the chickens sitting in the pond.

Chooks in the _____

splish _____

clack _____

flip _____

chook _____

Glossary

chooks: chickens

roosting rail: a rail where birds rest

squat: bend down

croon: sing

primp: fluff up

preen: make feathers lie flat

strut: walk proudly

verse: a section of a poem

⭐ Challenge yourself!

1 Look at the rhyme. Find the words that tell you:

a where the chickens are

b the noises the chickens make

c how the chickens show off.

2 The chickens are going to sleep. Write the verse using these words:

(rustling)　(resting)　(clucking)　(nesting)

Start your verse: (Chooks in the coop _____)

A lullaby from China

Learn

A **poem** is a picture with words. Poets use interesting words in their poems.

> Little silver moon rides the sky like a boat …

We can write interesting words we read and use them in our own poems.

silver moon

Get started!

1 Pretend you are lying in bed at night. You are looking at a crescent moon moving across the starry sky. Listen and read this rhyme from China.

> It is a lullaby. A lullaby is a song sung at bedtime to help you get to sleep.

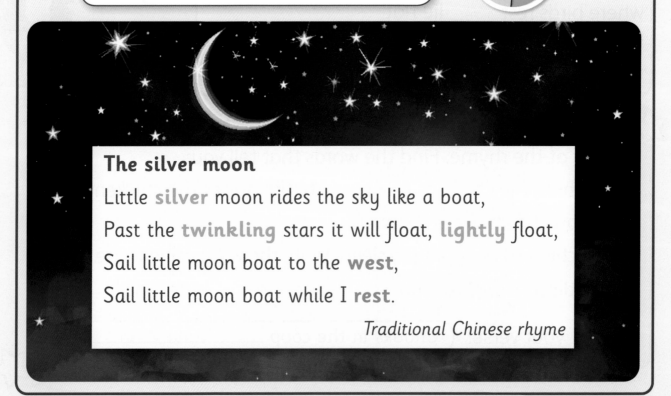

The silver moon

Little **silver** moon rides the sky like a boat,

Past the **twinkling** stars it will float, **lightly** float,

Sail little moon boat to the **west**,

Sail little moon boat while I **rest**.

Traditional Chinese rhyme

2 What is the rhyme about? How is the moon like a boat? Tell your partner and listen to your partner's ideas.

> The moon is the shape of a boat. The moon-boat is floating across the sky.

3 Read the words shown in orange in the rhyme. Use them to complete these lines:

   a Little _____ moon

   b the _____ stars

   c _____ float

4 Think about the moon and the stars at night. Tell your partner what they look like.

> Do you know any other lullabies?

5 Draw a picture of the moon and stars. Write words around the edge of your picture to describe the moon and stars.

Use these interesting words from the rhyme or your own ideas, for example: *twinkling dots* or *a silver smile*.

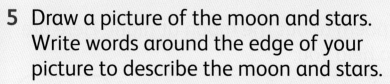

(silver) (little) (floating)

(lightly) (twinkling)

6 Learn the rhyme off by heart. Say it aloud to the class.

Glossary
twinkling: flashing
lightly: gently
rest: lie in bed
west: the part of the sky where the sun sets

Go further

1 Look at this picture of a full moon.

   a What does it look like? (Perhaps *a ball, a balloon, an eye watching you sleep* or *a lamp to light your room*?) What colour is it?

   b Share your ideas with a partner.

2 Use these words to write about the moon and stars:

glowing bright silver starry gold

watching light ball peep sleep

Challenge yourself!

1 Write a short rhyming poem about the moon at night. Here are some rhyming words to help you:

light – bright ball – fall peep – sleep eye – sky

balloon – spoon look – book

2 Read your poem to a partner. Tell your partner what you like about your poem. Tell them what you like about their poem.

Science

1 Find out about the night sky where you live. Can you see stars? If not, why not?

2 Some of the stars in the sky are actually planets. Find out the names of the planets that are close to the Earth.

A kite rhyme from Japan

Do you remember?

A **verb** is a doing word. A **noun** is a person, a place or a thing.

noun	verb

↓ ↓

*The **wind blows**.*

noun	verb	noun

↓ ↓ ↓

*The **girl holds** the **string**.*

noun	verb	noun

↓ ↓ ↓

*The **wind pulls** the **string**.*

Get started!

1 Listen and point to this rhyme from Japan. Join in.

Glossary
rising: going up
soaring: going high
height: being high up in the sky

Song of kites

Our kite is **rising** in the sky
Playful winds will take it high
Soaring, dancing higher yet
Up where clouds are floating by.
Falling, falling is the kite
Run and run to give it **height**
See, our kite is rising now
Don't forget to hold on tight.

Traditional Japanese poem

2 Find and point to these nouns in the poem:

(kite) (sky) (winds) (clouds)

3 Find and point to these verbs in the poem:

(rising) (soaring) (dancing) (falling) (hold)

Can you spot these spelling patterns? (ou) (oa)

4 Write a sentence as if you are the kite. You could use one of these sentence starters:

- I am dancing _____.
- I am playing _____.

Look at the poem for useful words.

5 Draw a picture of a kite.
Write a short poem using the nouns and verbs from the poem.

I am _____.   I am _____.
I am _____.   I am _____.

Remember to use a full stop and a capital letter for **I**.

Go further

Choose an outdoor activity you like, such as *riding a bike* or *playing football*.

1 Write a list of verbs for your activity, such as *kicking*, *zooming* and *laughing*.

2 Write a list of nouns to do with the activity, such as *wheels*, *hair*, *ball*, *feet* and *grass*.

3 Write a list poem for an activity. For example:

Wheels turning

Hair flying

Feet whizzing

Challenge yourself!

1 Choose your favourite poem from this unit and read it again. Tell a partner why you like it.

2 Create a performance of the poem you chose.
- Try to use your voice to make the poem fun to listen to.
- Say some lines slow.
- Say some lines fast.

You could add some actions!

What can you do?

Read and review what you can do.
- ✔ I can spell the numbers one to ten.
- ✔ I can find and say words that rhyme.
- ✔ I can form my letters in the correct way.
- ✔ I can say the alphabet from **a** to **z**.
- ✔ I can use interesting words in my poems.
- ✔ I can find a noun in a poem.
- ✔ I can find a verb in a poem.

Now you know some rhymes from around the world.

Quiz 1

1 One word in each sentence is missing its capital letter. Write the word correctly.

   a it was hot.

   b Today, suzy is five.

   c We live in shanghai.

   d Toby and i are best friends.

2 Write the two words that are nouns.

   (hat)   (jump)   (run)   (bag)

3 Write the two words that are verbs.

   (chair)   (cloud)   (sing)   (jog)

4 Use the words to finish the recount.

   (Finally)   (Next)   (First)

> Yesterday, we went to the seaside.
>
> _____, we played in the sand.
>
> Then we had our lunch.
>
> _____, we had an ice cream.
>
> _____, we went home.

5 Write the word that rhymes with each word below.

   (blend)   (bin)   (sat)

   tin   hat   send

6 Choose the correct word in each line that matches the picture. Then count the number of objects and write the number.

a   hat   hats   ☐

b   ducks   duck   ☐

c   mugs   mug   ☐

d   brush   brushes   ☐

e   box   boxes   ☐

7 Write the correct spelling of the word.

   a Tell me which/wich cake you want.

   b Pip waz/was on her way to school.

   c My teacher said/saed well done.

   d Sam took off/of her coat.

   e Jon lost his/hiz scarf.

8 Write the word next to its meaning.

   (jingling)   (squawk)   (twinkling)   (squat)

   (flashing)   (bend down)   (screech)   (ringing)

9 What sort of writing is each one?

   (poem)   (fantasy story)   (recount)

   a One day, a blimp and a bong were flying over the squash marshes.

   b Last week, we went to the library.

   c On a cold, dark night
     The stars shine bright.

The ungrateful tiger

Learn

A **traditional tale** is a very old story.

- Each country has its own traditional tales.
- Traditional tales often teach us how to behave.

Have you read any traditional tales?

Do you remember?

The people or animals in a story are called the **characters**.

Many traditional tales have animals as their main characters.

The **main characters** are the most important people or animals in the story.

Get started!

1 Listen and point to this traditional tale from Korea. Who are the main characters?

The ungrateful tiger

Once upon a time, Tiger lived in the deep jungle. One day, when Tiger was searching for food, he slipped and he fell into a deep, muddy trap.

He struggled and he struggled but he could not get out. Every time he climbed up the side of the trap, he slipped back to the bottom. He cried for help. Days went by and Tiger became hungry and scared.

At last, a man heard Tiger's cry. Without wasting a minute, the man lowered a

branch into the ditch. Tiger crawled up over the branch and jumped out.

At once, Tiger – who was very hungry – grabbed the man in his jaws.

'What are you doing?' cried the man. 'I have just saved your life!'

'Sorry,' Tiger replied, 'I need to eat.'

2 How do we know the man is kind? Copy the correct answer.

   a He cries when he sees Tiger in trouble.

   b He lets Tiger eat him.

   c He helps Tiger without thinking about the danger.

3 Talk to your partner about the story.

   a What do you think Tiger will do next? Why?

   b Do you think Tiger is bad? Why?

4 Act out the story with a partner. Tell your partner how your character feels at each point in the story.

Glossary
ungrateful: not showing thanks for something done for you by another person
trap: long, deep hole

Go further

1 Write a sentence for each picture.

a

b

c

Look in the story for useful words for your sentences and to help with spelling.

Have you used a capital letter and a full stop for each sentence?

2 Can you think of another ending for the story? Draw a picture for your end of the story. Write some sentences.

Challenge yourself!

1 Write what you would say to Tiger. Explain to Tiger why it is bad to eat the man.

2 Copy and complete the sentences.

a Tiger feels _____ when he is in the ditch.

b The man feels _____ when he sees Tiger.

c The man feels _____ and _____ when Tiger tries to eat him.

Did you know?

The Bengal tiger lives in India. Many people work to protect it.

Every tiger has its own pattern of stripes.

The trick

Do you remember?

We can use the word **and** to join **ideas** together.

> Tiger is scared **and** hungry.

We can use **and** to join **sentences** together.

> Tiger slips in the mud. Tiger falls in the trap.

> Tiger slips in the mud **and** falls in the trap.

Learn

We tell **stories**:
- to make us laugh
- to take us on an adventure
- to make us think about others.

> Stories can teach us how to be kind, or how to be a good friend.

Get started!

1 Use the pictures to tell the beginning of *The ungrateful tiger*.

2 How do you think the man will escape? Discuss your ideas with a partner.

3 Listen and point to the end of the story.

Just then, Rabbit passed by and saw the man in danger. He asked what the matter was. The man explained how he had saved Tiger's life. Tiger growled and said, 'I will die if I don't eat. The man is my food.'

'Let me help,' said Rabbit. 'Tell me – where was Tiger?'

Tiger pointed at the trap. 'I was in there.'

'Where?' asked Rabbit. 'I can't see.'

Hungry Tiger was getting cross. 'Look,' he said, 'I will show you.' Tiger jumped back into the trap.

Quick as a flash, Rabbit and the man pulled the branch out of the trap.

Poor Tiger was once again back in the deep trap, licking his paw and listening to his stomach rumbling.

4 What does **quick as a flash** mean? Write the answer.

> *Quick as a flash*, Rabbit and the man pulled the branches out of the trap.

   a   very fast

   b   secretly

   c   in the sunshine

5 Copy one sentence from the story that uses **and**. With your partner, say which two ideas **and** joins.

6 Copy and complete these sentences.

   a Tiger is _____ and _____ .

   b Rabbit is _____ and _____ .

7 Read these questions. Tell your partner the answer.

   a Why does Rabbit trick Tiger to get him back in the trap?

   b Why does Tiger attack the man?

Go further

1 Which of these sentences do you agree with? Tell your partner. Explain your answer. Listen to your partner's ideas.

   a Rabbit was wrong to trick Tiger.

   b Tiger deserved to be tricked.

   c Tiger might die now.

   d The man was wrong to help Tiger.

   e We should be kind to people who help us.

   f A tiger cannot help eating people.

2 What do you think the story is trying to teach us? Write the message of the story.

> Perhaps the story is telling us to be thankful to people who help us!

Challenge yourself!

1 Imagine Tiger is telling the story to his mother. Act out the conversation with a partner.

> Remember to use a capital letter for the word **I**.

2 Write the story Tiger tells his mother. Use the word **and** at least three times in your story.

3 Write what Tiger's mother says to him. Is she cross with him, or cross with Rabbit?

Tiddalik the Thirsty Frog

Do you remember?

We can often tell what someone is feeling by looking at their face.

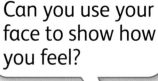
Can you use your face to show how you feel?

I am happy.

I am sad.

I am worried.

Learn

A **setting** is the place where a story happens.

A story setting could be:

- a forest
- a city
- in space
- under the sea.

Get started!

1 Follow and point to the opening of this traditional tale from Australia.

Tiddalik, the Thirsty Frog

Long ago, in **Dreamtime**, when the world was new, there lived a small frog called Tiddalik. The hot sun made him thirsty, so Tiddalik hopped down to the **waterhole** for a drink.

Tiddalik drank and drank until the waterhole was dry, but he was still thirsty. So, he drank all the water in the **creek**, the **billabongs**, the swamps, the rivers and the **lagoons** – until there wasn't a drop left. After he'd finished, Tiddalik's belly was as huge as a mountain and he was too heavy to hop anywhere.

There was no water for the other animals to drink. They **pleaded** with Tiddalik for water, but he kept his mouth shut.

'Let's make him laugh,' suggested **Wombat**.

'Good idea,' said **Kookaburra** and she told some jokes. But Tiddalik didn't even smile.

A traditional Australian story by Angela McAllister

A Year Full of Stories, written by Angela McAllister and illustrated by Christopher Corr*, published by Frances Lincoln Children's Books, an imprint of The Quarto Group, copyright © 2016. Reproduced by permission of Quarto Publishing Plc.

Glossary

Dreamtime: in Australian stories, the time at the beginning of the world

waterhole: a small pond where animals drink

creek: a small river

billabongs: ponds

lagoons: lakes

pleaded: begged

wombat: a small bear-like animal

kookaburra: a large Australian bird

2 Read these words from the story.

(Tiddalik) (thirsty) (waterhole)

(Wombat) (Kookaburra)

What do the words mean? Tell your partner.

3 Discuss these questions with your partner.

   a Who is the main character?

   b When does the story take place?

   c Why does Tiddalik drink all the water?

   d Why are the animals cross with Tiddalik?

4 a What do the characters feel when Tiddalik drinks the water? Write a sentence. Choose two of these words:

(happy) (worried) (uninterested)

(cross) (sad)

   b Act out the feelings. Ask your partner to guess the feeling. Swap roles.

Go further

1 Work in groups of four and act out the story. Use your face to show how your character feels.

2 In your group, take turns as your character to answer questions about how you feel after Tiddalik has drunk all the water. Take turns to ask questions of the other characters. When you answer, use your face to show how you feel.

Challenge yourself!

Write a note to Tiddalik telling him to share his water. Explain why it is important. Use these words:

(fair) (water)

(share) (thirsty)

(worried) (sad)

Tiddalik shares

Get started!

1 Do you remember the beginning of *Tiddalik, the Thirsty Frog*? Use these pictures to tell your partner:

ⓐ    ⓑ    ⓒ

2 Listen and read the end of the story.

Koala stood on her head, **Echidna** made funny faces and Lizard danced a silly dance – but still Tiddalik sat with his lips closed tight.

Last to try was Kangaroo, who **boxed** with his shadow, thump, thump, thump! The thumping **disturbed Platypus** who'd been sleeping nearby.

'Who woke me up?' she said, snapping her beak. Tiddalik stared in surprise, he'd never seen such a **weird** looking creature.

Platypus banged her tail and tapped her webbed feet crossly, 'Well, what's going on?' The angrier she got, the more **ridiculous** she looked.

At last, Tiddalik couldn't help himself, he opened his mouth to laugh.

'Watch out!' cried Wombat.

Out **gushed** a great flood, filling the waterholes and creeks, the billabongs and swamps and lagoons; plenty enough for all the animals to drink.

By Angela McAllister

3 Find verbs ending in **ed** in the story. Copy five verbs.

> These letters show that the action took place in the past.

4 Find these verbs in the story:

(gushed) (danced) (boxed)

Tell your partner what these words mean.

5 How do the animals try and make Tiddalik laugh? Tell your partner. How would you make Tiddalik laugh? Copy and complete the sentence.

I would _____.

6 What did Platypus do when she was angry? Write down two things.

7 Write these sentences in the correct order. Add two more sentences to finish the story.

> Kangaroo woke up Platypus.
>
> Tiddalik drank all the water.
>
> Lizard danced a silly dance.
>
> The animals pleaded with Tiddalik.

8 Write a sentence describing the platypus.

Glossary

koala: a furry animal that looks like a small bear and lives in trees

echidna: a small animal with spiny fur

boxed: fought

disturbed: woke up

platypus: a furry animal with a beak and webbed feet

weird: strange

ridiculous: very silly

gushed: ran out quickly

Go further

1 What lesson does the story teach us? Tell your partner.

Does the story teach us about sharing?

2 Write a sentence for each picture.

 (a)

 (b)

 (c)

 (d)

3 Draw a picture for the ending. Write a sentence for your picture. Use these useful words:

laughed   boxed   gushed   drank   pleaded

Challenge yourself!

1 Read the text on page 74 to your partner.

Can you show Tiddalik with his tight lips? Can you show Platypus looking angry?

2 What do you think happened after Tiddalik laughed up all the water? Write what happened next.

In your story, will Tiddalik learn his lesson? How will the animals stop Tiddalik drinking the water again?

Art

This Australian picture is painted using dots. Use paint dots of different colours to create a picture of Tiddalik.

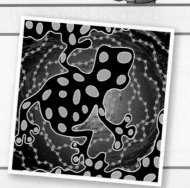

The King of the Forest

Do you remember?

The **beginning**, **middle** and **end** are different parts of a story.

Beginning: We meet the character. An adventure starts.

> Tiddalik drinks all the water.

Middle: The main part of the story.

> The animals try and make Tiddalik laugh.

End: The story finishes.

> Tiddalik sees Platypus and laughs out all the water.

Get started!

1   Listen and point to this traditional tale from China.

King of the Forest

Tiger King Bole was taking a **nap** under a tree in his forest when suddenly he woke up. A nut had hit him on the head! He saw Squirrel Cuka standing on a branch and throwing pine nuts at him.

'Quick! Quick! There's a snake!' Squirrel Cuka called, pointing to the bushes.

There was a boa making **rustling** noises in the bushes. Bole jumped up and chased him away.

Tiger King Bole said 'thank you' and they soon became good friends.

Cuka could climb high up in the trees and see what was happening in the open grasslands. He told Tiger King Bole everything he saw.

'Oh no! I can see Red Fox Rex coming this way with Lion King Te!'

'Why are they coming here? The forest is my kingdom, and I am the King! Everyone knows that!' said Tiger King Bole.

'Yes, but Red Fox Rex wants his friend, Lion King Te to be King of the Forest and King of the Grassland. Lion King Te isn't good at climbing trees and swimming, not like you!'

Tiger King Bole was very angry and wanted to fight Lion King Te. The eagles in the trees flapped their huge wings and went to tell Lion King Te.

'I will fight him and become the King of the Forest and King of the Grassland,' **roared** Lion King Te, when the eagles told him.

The next day, Tiger King Bole and Lion King Te came face to face on the top of a very high mountain. From the top of mountain, waterfalls **cascaded** down to the deep **gorge** below. There was a rock pool and the river water thrashed against the sides, making the water bubbly and frothy as it twisted and turned.

Lion King Te pounced at Tiger King Bole with a mighty roar and with his huge teeth and sharp claws outstretched and ready to attack, but Tiger King Bole was too fast and jumped to the side. Squirrel Cuka and Red Fox Rex gasped in horror as Lion King Te disappeared over the waterfall and fell into the water with a huge SPLASH!

Everyone waited and waited for Lion King Te to come to the **surface**, but there was nothing … no bubbles, no sign of life.

Tiger King Bole called the crocodiles to find Lion King Te and pull him out of the water.

'Thank you,' said Lion King Te as he lay on the rocks. 'You saved my life. I am sorry I tried to fight you. You are King of the Forest and I am King of the Grassland, and although we are different, we can still live beside each other in peace and harmony. There is no need to fight.'

'Yes, this is true,' said Tiger King Bole. 'We can also maybe learn from each other. I can teach you how to swim and maybe you could teach me to sharpen my claws?'

'Of course! Anything for a friend!' said his new friend and King of the Grassland.

Glossary

nap: a short sleep, especially during the day

rustling: making a soft, muffled crackling sound, like walking on dry leaves

roared: the noise a lion makes

cascaded: to pour down very quickly and in large quantities

gorge: a narrow valley between hills or mountains, usually with steep, rocky walls and a stream running through it

surface: the top of the water

2 Talk to your partner about the story.

   a Who are the two main characters in the story?

   b Why did Tiger King Bole and Lion King Te fight?

   c How did Tiger King Bole win the fight?

3 What does **pounced** mean? Choose the best answer.

(moved slowly towards) (walked quickly) (jumped on to catch)

4 With a partner, read these events from the story and write them in a table like the one below.

Put two events into each section.

> Lion King Te and Tiger King Bole meet at the top of a waterfall.
>
> Squirrel Cuka throws a pine nut at Tiger King Bole.
>
> The eagles tell Lion King Te that Tiger King Bole wants to fight.
>
> Lion King Te falls over the waterfall into the water below.
>
> Lion King Te and Tiger King Bole become friends.
>
> Squirrel Cuka and Tiger King Bole become friends.

Beginning	Middle	End

Go further

Look at the table you created for *The King of the Forest*. Use this to help you act out the story with your group.

1 Decide who will play the different characters in the story. Talk about your ideas and what the different characters say and do before you act it out.

2 Remember to use your face and body language to show what the characters are thinking and feeling.

⭐ Challenge yourself!

Design a book cover for *The King of the Forest* story. Decide what will go on the front cover and what will go on the back cover. Where will you put the title?

Let me tell you a story

Learn

We can start stories in many ways:

- *Once upon a time …*
- *Long ago, in Dreamtime …*
- *Long, long ago …*
- *There once was …*
- *One day …*

These phrases tell us that we are about to hear a story.

We can use story language to keep a story going:

- *Quick as a flash, …*
- *In the blink of an eye, …*
- *All at once, …*
- *After a little while, …*
- *Before long, …*

These phrases tell us how something happened.

Get started!

1 Make up your own traditional tale! You will need two animals and a problem. Here are some ideas – or you could use your own.

Frog sings and frightens the fish Turtle wants to eat.

Turtle tricks Frog into eating stones.

Frog croaks. Turtle is sad.

2 Plan the beginning of your story using a table like this:

		Words I will use
Main characters	Turtle Frog	snapping crooning singing grumbling
Beginning	Turtle and frog are friends. Frog sings all day and keeps fish away. Turtle gets hungry.	Once upon a time, there was …

3 Tell your partner about your story beginning.

Which words will start your story?

Look at the list of story phrases in the *Learn* panel for ideas.

Go further

1 Talk to your partner about what could happen in the middle and end of the story. Listen to your partner's ideas.

2 Complete the plan for the story. Write notes in your table for the beginning, the middle and the end.

		Words I will use
Middle	Turtle tells Frog to stop. He doesn't. Turtle gives Frog a big meal. He stops for a while then swallows. Turtle tricks Frog into eating stones.	Before long … At last …
End	Frog can only croak. Turtle misses singing.	Now …

3 Tell your story to a partner.

- Ask your partner to tell you what they liked about your story.
- Ask them to tell you which parts need to change.

4 Change one thing in your plan to make your story better.

5 Tell your story to another partner.

Look at your partner as you tell your story to see if they are enjoying it. If they look interested, put in more detail. If they look bored, move on to the next part of the story.

Challenge yourself!

Practise telling your story. Here are some ideas to make your story fun to listen to:

- Move around as you talk.
- Sit on a special storytelling chair.
- Show what the animals feel with your face.
- Bang on a drum to start and finish your story.

Geography

1 The stories in this unit come from India, China and Australia. Find these countries on a map of the world or on a globe.

2 Find out which continents each of these countries are in.

3 Find out which seas or oceans are near these countries.

Write it down

Learn

We can collect **interesting words** that we come across.

We can use these words in our own stories.

Can you find interesting words in the stories in this unit?

Get started!

1   We have read some great verbs in this unit. Choose two verbs that you could use in your own traditional tale.

Super verbs!					
thrashed	pleaded	pounced	rumbled	cascaded	twisted
banged	boxed	snapping	gushed	struggled	crawled

2   Draw three large circles like this. Write verbs you have chosen for your story in the circles. Two examples have been done for you.

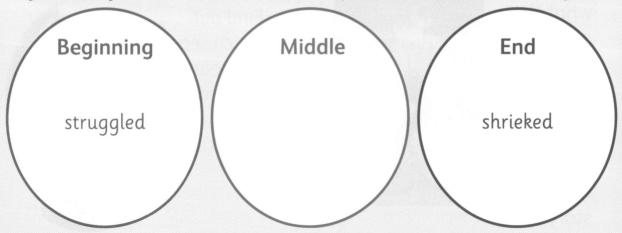

Beginning

struggled

Middle

End

shrieked

3 Go on a word hunt in this unit. Write two words you want to use in each circle.

4 Retell your story to a new partner. Use your new words.

5 Draw two pictures to show the beginning of your story. Write some sentences for each picture to tell the story.
Use one of these story openers to start your story:

- *Once upon a time, …*
- *Long ago, …*
- *Long, long ago, …*
- *There once was …*
- *One day, …*

Check you have used the verbs from your circles on page 84.

Remember to use capital letters and full stops.

Go further

1 Draw pictures for the middle and the end of your story. Write sentences for each picture to tell the story.

2 Make one sentence longer by using **and**.

3 Read your story to a partner. Pause at the end of each sentence to make the story easy to follow.

Remember to use the words and ideas from your story plan.

⭐ Challenge yourself!

1 Check the spelling of the new words in your story.

2 Look at the words you have used. Can you use one or two more interesting verbs from the list on page 84?

> Ask your teacher to help you check the spelling of new words.

3 Read your story aloud to yourself. Check that it makes sense. Add one of these phrases to your story:

- *Quick as a flash, …*
- *In the blink of an eye, …*
- *All at once, …*
- *After a little while, …*
- *Before long, …*

4 Read your story to a partner. Tell your partner about your favourite part of the story. Ask your partner what they liked about the story.

What can you do?

Read and review what you can do.

> Now you know some traditional stories from around the world.

- ✔ I can talk about the character in a story.
- ✔ I can use **and** to join ideas together.
- ✔ I can talk about the setting of a story.
- ✔ I can check that each sentence has a verb.
- ✔ I can find and use verbs ending in **ed**.
- ✔ I can use some phrases to add detail to my story.
- ✔ I can collect interesting words from the stories I read.
- ✔ I can talk about what happens in the beginning, middle and end of a story.
- ✔ I can use some story openers to start a story.

Do this! Do that!

Instructions can be used for a list, a sign or a recipe! An instruction tells you to do something.

Instructions have:

- clear sentences
- **bossy verbs** that start the sentence
- numbers that show the order
- pictures or **diagrams**.

> A **bossy verb** orders you to do something such as *go*, *jump*, *sit* and *run*.

bossy verb

1 **Break** the eggs.

number

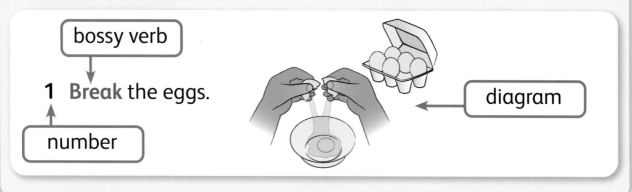

diagram

1 Which sign is an instruction? Why?

a **156**

b **Zara**

c **WASH YOUR HANDS**

2 What is each instruction telling you to do? Tell your partner.

Hang up your coat.

To do
Bake a cake.
Tidy the house.
Make the sandwiches.
Lay the table.
Blow up the balloons.

How to use a balloon pump

1 Put the balloon over the **nozzle**.

2 Pull the **base** of the pump in and out.

3 Take the balloon off the pump. Tie a knot.

3 With a partner, point to the instruction that:

a   is a list of chores (jobs)

b   has pictures

c   tells you how to do something

d   has numbers

e   is a sign

f   tells you what to do.

4 Write a sign for this picture. Use the words to help you.

litter   bin

put

Glossary
nozzle: the tip of the pump where the air comes out
base: bottom

Go further

1 Give your partner these instructions. Tell your partner to do the action *only* when a bossy verb is given.

   a You are jumping.   b Sit.

   c You can walk.   d You can stand.

   e Jump.   f Run.

2 Use bossy verbs to order your partner around for one minute! Ask your partner to do actions like these:

   - *Touch your nose.*
   - *Stand on one leg.*
   - *Jump six times.*

3 Rewrite these sentences as instructions. The first one has been done for you.

   a You will go to school. Go to school.   b You will sit down.

   c You will write neatly.   d You will play nicely at lunch.

Challenge yourself!

What do you need to remember to do in the morning?

- Write yourself a *To do* list.
- Use bossy verbs.

To do
Make my bed.
Find my shoes.
Brush my hair.
Eat breakfast.

Did you know?

The instructions of Shuruppak are one of the oldest pieces of writing in the world. They are a set of instructions from a king to his son telling him how to behave!

Following instructions in order

Learn

Many **instructions** must be done in the correct order. **Numbers** or **time words** help.

Time words
- → *First*, go to the library.
- → *Then*, go to the *bakery*.
- → *Finally*, meet me at the car.

Numbers
- → **1** *Turn right outside school.*
- → **2** *Walk to the corner.*
- → **3** *Cross the road at the lights.*

> **Numbers** and **time words** make the instructions easy to follow.

Get started!

Glossary
bakery: a shop that sells bread

1 Look at this map. Follow the instructions to find Ana's house.

Be careful crossing the road!

1 First, walk out of the school and turn right onto the High Street.
2 Then, turn right at the crossroads at the bakery.
3 Next, go straight on past the park.
4 Finally, cross the road at the traffic lights.

left   right

2 Find and copy all the time words in the instructions on page 90.

3 Find and copy these direction words. Check your spelling.

(right) (straight on) (past)

4 Show your partner how you found Ana's house.

5 Look at this set of instructions for getting from Ana's house to Mateo's house on the map. Write the instructions in order.

- Then, turn right at the crossroads.
- First, turn right onto Park Street.
- Finally, look for the house with the red door.

Go further

With your partner, use the map on page 90, and write a set of instructions to walk from Ana's house to the bike shop. Can you use some of these words?

(First) (Next) (Then) (Finally)

★ Challenge yourself!

Look at the map on page 90. Mateo's bike is broken. Write a set of instructions to help him take the bike from the school to the bike shop to be fixed.

Geography

1 Look at a map of the roads around your school. Look for places that you pass on the way to school.

2 How would you walk from your school to the shops?

Nouns and bossy verbs

Do you remember?

Instructions use bossy words.

- **Bossy verbs** order you to do something.
- **Bossy verbs** help to make instructions easy to follow.

Do you like to choose books with instructions? Or do you prefer storybooks?

bossy verbs	→	*Put* soil in the pot.
	→	*Push* the seed into the soil.
	→	*Water* your pot every day.

Make, **jump**, **fold** and **slice** are all bossy verbs!

The **nouns** in instructions are the particular things that you need to do the task.

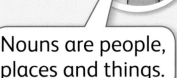

Nouns are people, places and things.

noun	noun

*Push the **seed** deep in the **soil**.*

Get started!

1 Pretend you are telling someone how to plant a seed.

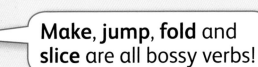

Remember to use bossy verbs!

Give your partner instructions and ask them to pretend to be doing the actions.

2 Listen and point to these instructions. Were your instructions on page 92 similar? Look out for the bossy verbs!

How to grow a sunflower

What you need:

a plant pot   some **soil**

a sunflower seed   a watering can

What to do:

1 Fill the pot with soil.

2 Push the seed into the soil.

3 Put the pot on a sunny **windowsill**.

4 Check the pot every day and water it if the soil feels dry.

5 Plant the sunflower outside when the **shoot** grows into a plant.

6 Watch the sunflower grow tall, with a yellow flower.

3 Find and copy two bossy verbs.

4 Find and copy three nouns.

> The bossy verb usually comes at the beginning of a sentence.

Glossary

soil: earth for growing things

windowsill: the shelf by a window

shoot: a tiny plant

Global Perspectives Challenge: Learning new things

Learning a new skill

Think about a time you learned something new by following instructions. Tell a partner:

• what you learned

• who taught you the new thing

• how you do the new thing.

Go further

Copy and complete the instructions. Use these bossy verbs:

(Draw) (Sprinkle) (Stick) (Fill) (Cut)

You will need:
- **cress** seeds
- a pot
- paper and pens
- glue
- scissors

What to do:

1 _____ the pot with soil.

2 _____ the cress seeds on the soil.

3 _____ a funny face on the paper.

4 _____ out the funny face.

5 _____ the face on the pot.

6 Wait for the cress to grow like hair!

⭐ Challenge yourself!

Sunflower seeds can make great food for birds. Use these bossy verbs and useful nouns to write instructions to go with these pictures.

[1]

(wait) (cut) (hang) (throw) (sunflower) (seeds)

(fork) (outside) (birds) (dry) (remove)

[2]

[3]

[4]

[5]

Glossary
cress: a fast-growing, edible herb

Make a present

Do you remember?

A **noun** is a person, a place or a thing.
Glue, **pens**, **paper**, **card** and **scissors** are all nouns.

Get started!

1 Listen and point. How do the pictures help you to understand what to do?

How to make a pom-pom keyring

You will need:
- a small ball of wool
- a keyring chain
- two rings of card
- scissors

What to do:

First, tie the end of the wool to the ring of card. Next, wind the wool around the ring. **1**	Keep winding the wool around the ring. Then, cut and tie the end to the wool in the middle. **2**
Next, cut around the edges of the ring. **3**	Then cut a piece of wool. **Thread** the chain through the wool. Wind the wool around the middle twice. **4**
Next, tie the wool tight. Cut out the card. Finally fluff up the pom-pom. **5**	**Glossary** **pom-pom**: a small woollen ball **thread**: to put through

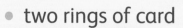

2 Find and copy from the text on page 95:

    a an item from the *You will need* list

    b three bossy verbs

    c three nouns

    d two time words.

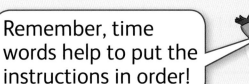 

Remember, time words help to put the instructions in order!

3 Look at the instructions. Find and write the missing nouns.

    a First tie the end of the _____ to the rings of card.

    b Cut out the _____.

Go further

1 Work with a partner. You will each need some beads and a piece of string.

- Secretly, use some beads to make a bracelet.

- Now, give your partner instructions to make the same bracelet. For example, you could say:

> **1** *First, tie a knot in the string.*
> **2** *Then, thread two red beads onto the string.*
> **3** *Next, thread two yellow beads onto the string.*

- Compare bracelets. Do they match?

2 Copy and complete the instructions. Use these words:

string   beads   tie   thread   one   two

three   four   red   blue   green   piece

How to make a bracelet
What to do:
1 First, thread _____ _____ beads on the string.
2 Then, thread _____ .
3 Next, _____ .
4 Finally, _____ the ends of the _____ .

You will need:
• a _____ of string
• some _____

Challenge yourself!

1 How do you think this handprint spider was made? Write a set of instructions. Remember to use:
  • a *What you will need* list
  • numbers
  • pictures
  • bossy verbs (such as *paint*, *press*, *wait*, *glue* and *cut*)
  • time words (such as *first*, *next* and *then*).

2 Check your instructions by reading them to a partner.

Design and Technology

1 Read the instructions on page 95 again and make a pom-pom keyring.

2 Tell your partner how you made it.

More instructions

Do you remember?

English words are made from **vowels** and **consonants**.

vowel
↓
c-a-t
↑ ↑
consonants

| The vowels are: | The consonants are: |

The vowels are:

| a | e | i | o | u |

The consonants are:

| b | c | d | f | g | h | j | k | l | m | n |
| p | q | r | s | t | v | w | x | y | z |

We can use **a** or **an** before a noun.
- We use **a** when the next word begins with a **consonant**.

*Here is **a c**ake.*

- We use **an** when the noun starts with a **vowel**.

*Here is **an e**gg.*

Learn

We can use **adverbs** to show **how** something should be done.

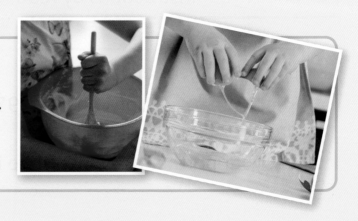

- *Stir the mixture **quickly**.*
- *Break the eggs **carefully**.*

Get started!

1 Read these instructions. Point to the bossy verbs, time words, pictures, numbers and the *You will need* list.

How to bake party cakes

What to do:

1 First, heat the oven to 190 **degrees**.

2 Mix the butter and sugar.

3 Add the eggs.

4 Gently stir in the flour and baking powder.

5 Put the mixture in the cases.

6 Carefully put the cakes in the oven. Ask an adult to help you.

7 Bake the cakes for 20 minutes.

You will need:
two eggs
100 g butter
100 g sugar
100 g flour
half teaspoon baking powder
12 paper cases
baking tray

2 Find and copy nouns that are used to make cakes, such as **eggs** and **sugar**.

3 With a partner, pretend to make the cakes. Use the words that are special for making cakes.

4 Choose **a** or **an**. Write the word.

a _____ egg

b _____ cake

c _____ tin

d _____ tray

e Ask _____ adult to help you.

f Use _____ pair of oven gloves.

We use **an** when the noun starts with a vowel.

Glossary

degrees: the measurement used for temperature

100 g: 100 grams

baking powder: a powder that helps cakes to rise

paper cases: paper holders for cupcakes and muffins

Go further

1 Find and copy two words from the instructions on page 99 that tell you how something should be done.

Hint: These words will end in **ly**.

2 Write an instruction for each picture below to show how to ice and decorate the cakes. Use these words:

(water) (icing sugar) (bowl) (jug) (spoon)

(mix) (knife) (spread) (sprinkles) (cakes)

①
②
③

Challenge yourself!

1 What is your favourite party food? Find out how to make it.

2 Write the instructions. Remember to use:
- bossy verbs
- a list of things you need
- pictures
- numbered points
- time words.

What can you do?

Read and review what you can do.

✔ I can find the bossy verbs in an instruction.

✔ I can follow instructions step by step.

✔ I can give clear instructions to a friend.

✔ I can use **a** or **an** correctly.

✔ I can use time words or numbers when writing instructions.

Now you can read and write instructions.

Unit 6 Poetry: Simple rhyming poems

A rainy day

Do you remember?

Try and join some letters together.
This can make it easier to write.

sh   ch   ck   tl   nk

Check that you are holding your pencil correctly.

Learn

We can have fun with sounds in words.
We can have:

- words that rhyme   puddles – huddles
- words with similar sounds   trip – trop
- repeated words   rain, rain, rain, rain
- made-up words   chucketing

Get started!

1 Read this list of rain words.

splish   splash   glug   pour   gush   muddle   rush

flood   drizzle   mist   soak   drench   spots

mizzle   splodge   burst   thirst   mud   drops

floor   puddle   coat

2 Write pairs of words from question 1 that go together.

Your pairs of words can be:
- words that rhyme
- words that start with the same sound
- words that are repeated.

Choose words that rhyme or words that have matching sounds.

3 Read this poem.

Rain

One is one, and two is two –
we sing in **huddles**,
we hop in puddles.
Plip, plop,
we drip on rooftop,
trip, **trop**,
the rain will not stop.

Rain, rain, rain, rain,
bucketing rain,
chucketing rain,
rain, rain, rain,
rain,
wonderfully raw,
wet to the **core**!

By Sigbjørn Obstfelder
Translated by Sarah Jane Hails

4 a Find these words in the poem. Read the lines.

- (huddles puddles)
- (bucketing chucketing)
- (rain rain)

b Which pairs of words rhyme? Which pair of words is the same? Which words are made up? Tell your partner.

Glossary
huddles: small groups
trop: a made-up word to make a rain sound
bucketing: raining very hard
chucketing: a made-up word that means raining very hard
core: centre

5 What is it like when it rains where you live? Think of some words to describe the rain, for example:

Check that you are joining the letters correctly.

(light) (heavy) (pitter) (patter)

(pour) (drizzle) (soft) (hard) (warm) (cold)

a Write four words.

b Use the words above to complete this poem.

Share your words with your partner.

_____ rain

_____ rain

_____ rain

_____ rain

Go further

1 Draw a puddle like this. Write your rhyming words in the drops.

2 Read your picture poem to a partner. Tell your partner which pair of words you like best.

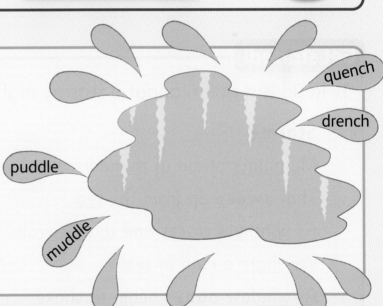

quench

drench

puddle

muddle

Challenge yourself!

Use the pairs of words from your picture poem to write a list poem. You can include:

- a rhyme, a made-up word and repeated words
- words that start with similar sounds.

Lightning crashes

Do you remember?

Words that **rhyme** often share a spelling pattern or sound. Look at these words:

> tea – sea   mat – cat   tray – say

Learn

We can look for **clues** to find out how somebody feels. For example:

- *if a boy is crying, he feels sad*
- *if a girl is smiling, she feels happy.*

Get started!

1   Read this poem about a stormy night. How does the girl feel?

Storms

My <u>mum's</u> afraid of <u>thun</u>derstorms
That **sweep** up from the <u>sea</u>.
As <u>lightning</u> cracks and <u>thunder</u> rolls
We <u>share</u> a mug of <u>tea</u>.
As <u>wind</u>ow **panes** be<u>gin</u> to shake
We like to watch T<u>V</u>.
My <u>mum's</u> afraid of <u>thun</u>derstorms
Ex<u>cept</u> when she's with <u>me</u>.

By Ron Simmons

Glossary

sweep: move quickly
panes: the glass in a window

2 Read the poem again and write the answers to these questions:

   a Where does the storm come from?

   b What noise does the lightning make?

   c Who is afraid of thunderstorms?

3 a Write the word that rhymes. Write both words.

   • sea _____

   • TV _____

   b Underline the words that have similar spelling.

4 With your partner:

   a Find words that tell you what the storm sounds like.

   b Decide if the words make the storm sound big or small.

   c Decide if the girl is afraid of the storm or not.

5 Read the poem again. Say the parts of the words that are underlined slightly louder to feel the rhythm.

Use your face to show that the storm is frightening.

Did you know?

It's raining fish!

In some countries, the storms are so bad that they actually rain fish! The storm sucks up fish from one place and rains them down in another. That is weird weather!

Go further

1   Look at these storm words. Find words that rhyme.

(shake) (shudder) (groans) (break) (judder) (pours)

(moans) (howls) (roars) (growls) (crashes) (flashes)

2   a   Copy and complete the poem.
Choose a word for each line.

In the storm

houses _____ (shake, shudder, flood)

trees_____ (break, judder, bend)

wind _____ (moans, howls, roars)

rain _____ (soaks, falls, pours)

lightning _____ (flashes, forks, breaks)

thunder _____ (crashes, cracks, rumbles)

> Look for words that share similar spelling patterns or sounds.

   b   Can you make some of the lines rhyme?

⭐ Challenge yourself!

1   Reread your poem. What do you think happens after the storm?
   • Does the sun come out?
   • Do the people have to clean up?
2   Write two more lines at the end of your poem, for example:

After the storm

The sun _____

Everyone _____

Hot, hot, hot

Learn

In poems, the lines that rhyme are not always next to each other.

The sun is hot

I cannot get cool

I think I will flop

Into the pool.

rhyme

Sometimes every other line rhymes.

Do you remember?

We use **a** when the next word begins with a *consonant*.

*This is **a** butterfly.*

*This is **an** ice cream.*

The consonants are: b c d f g h j k l m n p q r s t v w x y z

We use **an** when the noun starts with a vowel: a e i o u

Did you know?

The hottest place on the Earth is the Lut Desert in Iran.

Get started!

1 Imagine it is a very hot day. Read this poem.

The Dragonfly

When the heat of the summer
Made **drowsy** the land
A dragonfly came
And sat on my hand,
With its blue **jointed** body,
And wings like **spun glass**,
It **lit** on my fingers
As though they were grass.
By Eleanor Farjeon

2 Read the poem again. Find and copy the words that mean:
   a hot
   b sleepy

3 Use two of these words to write a sentence about the dragonfly.

   (fast)   (shiny)   (clear)   (green)   (gentle)

4 Write **a** or **an** to finish each sentence. Write the missing word.
   a It was _____ hot day.
   b I saw _____ ant in the grass.

5 Find these rhyming words in the poem:

   (glass – grass)   (show – slow)

6 Write another sentence saying how the dragonfly moves.

Glossary
drowsy: sleepy
jointed: with different parts
spun glass: thin glass
lit: sat on

Go further

1 Read this poem about a hot day.

Lemonade in the Shade

When the sun is
bright and hot

I like to find a
leafy spot

and cool off in
the shade.

It's nicer here
among the trees

where I can feel the
summer breeze

and sip my lemonade.

By Jodi Simpson

2 Tell your partner which poem you like best and why. Say which poem is most like the hot days you know.

3 Talk with your partner about what the girl is doing in the picture. How does she feel?

Challenge yourself!

Write a poem about a hot day. Here are some useful rhyming words:

(trees – breeze)   (hot – not)   (pool – cool)

(sleep – deep)   (scream – ice cream)

Let it snow

A good listener:
- looks at the person who is talking
- does not interrupt
- asks questions.

Look interested when people are talking to you.

Get started!

1 Have you ever seen snow? Did you know that snow can make the world very quiet? Read this poem.

Hush Now

The thing about snow is
It makes everything quiet –
Except, of course, for children
Snow just makes them **riot**.

By Mike Barfield

2 What is the poem about? Choose two things.
   a Children being noisy in the snow.
   b Snow causing trouble on the roads.
   c Snow making the world very quiet.

Glossary
riot: go wild

3 *Snow just makes them riot.* What does the word *riot* mean? Choose and copy the answer.

  a stay inside

  b play quietly

  c go wild

Look at the picture on page 110 for ideas.

4 Choose some words from question 3 to complete this sentence.

  The children _____ in the snow.

5 Look at these words. Find and copy two words that rhyme.

  quiet   children   riot

6 Read the poem aloud. Read the first part softly. Read the last line loudly.

Go further

1 Ask your partner:

  • Have you seen snow?

  • Do you like snow?

  • What would you do in the snow?

  • What could be bad about snow?

Remember to look at your partner when they are talking.

2 List your partner's answers like this:

  Suki wants to go skiing.
  Suki wants to make a snowman.
  Suki does not want to be cold.

Remember to listen to your partner's ideas.

3 a Reread the *Rain* poem on page 102.

b Ask your partner which poem they like best, *Rain* or *Hush Now*. Ask them to tell you why.

Make sure you have asked your partner to say why they like the poem.

⭐ Challenge yourself!

1 Write a poem listing different noises you would hear if you were watching the children play in the snow. Here are some noises to help you:

- *whoop thwack* (for a snowball)
- *swish swish* (skis)
- *whizz whee* (sledge)
- *scream yelp* (children)
- *creak crunch* (a snowman's body being rolled up)
- *clitter clatter* (ducks' feet on the ice)
- *drip drop* (icicles dripping).

Global Perspectives Challenge: Working together

Can you draw a picture for a favourite piece of music?

1 Listen to *Calling Snow,* a piece of music by Randy Granger. Close your eyes and imagine where you are and what you can smell. How does the music make you feel?

2 Together with your partner, decide on a scene that you are going to draw. Work together to draw a shared picture to go with the music.

It's raining hearts

Do you remember?

Verbs can end in **s**, **ing** and **ed**.

- *It is rain**ing**.*
- *I like it when it rain**s**.*
- *It rain**ed** yesterday.*

When we change the ending, we change the meaning.

Get started!

1 This poem is about all the nice things that could fall from the sky instead of rain or snow. Read the poem and listen out for all the different verbs.

It's Raining Hearts
It's raining hearts;
It's storming flowers;
We're in for **scattered**
Stardust showers.
It's **drizzling** chocolate,
Pouring pies;
We might be seeing
Candy skies.
Of all the weather
There could be,
Plain water seems
A waste to me.
By Barbara Vance

Glossary
scattered: a few here and there
stardust: tiny parts of stars
drizzling: raining lightly

2 Find and copy pairs of words in the poem that rhyme. Tell your partner the spelling of these words.

3 Draw a picture showing the different things falling from the sky.

- Add labels to your picture.

- Point to pairs of objects that rhyme.

4 Find verbs in the poem and look at their endings.

a _____ hearts

b _____ flowers

c _____ chocolate

d _____ pies

Most of the verbs in this poem end in **ing**.

5 Choose a poem from this unit to read again. Tell a partner why you chose it.

Go further

1 With a partner, talk about all the nice things that could fall instead of rain. Write a list.

2 Talk about the problems that could be caused by the different items falling.

3 Make up a spoken poem using your list. Use this to help you:

It's raining _____   It's drizzling _____

It's storming _____   It's pouring _____

We're in for scattered   We might be seeing

_____ showers.   _____ skies.

4 When you are happy with your poem, write it down. Draw a picture to go with the poem.

5 Share your poem in a small group. Ask them to tell you what they liked about your poem and what you could do to improve it.

Challenge yourself!

1 Read your poem again. Think of some different verbs to replace those in orange on page 114. For example, you could swap *raining* for *snowing*.

(raining) (storming) (drizzling) (pouring)

2 Make sure your verbs end in **ing**.

3 Write your poem again using the new verbs.

4 Read your poem to the class.

What can you do?

Read and review what you can do.

Now you know some weather poems.

✔ I can find words that rhyme in a poem.

✔ I can find words with similar sounds in a poem.

✔ I can join some letters when writing.

✔ I can work out how someone feels in a poem.

✔ I can see that some words that rhyme have similar spelling patterns.

✔ I can choose **a** or **an** correctly.

✔ I can be a good listener.

✔ I can find and read verbs ending in **ing**, **s** and **ed**.

1 a Write **beginning**, **middle** or **end** for each part of the story.

The sweet baby ducks were mean to the ugly duckling. He got very sad. He went and hid in the bushes. He slept in the bushes all summer.

Finally, the ugly duckling went back to the others. The sweet ducklings were now brown ducks. The ugly duckling was a beautiful swan.

Once upon a time, there were four ducklings. Three were very sweet. One was big and ugly. They lived on a lake with the mother duck.

b Who are the characters in the story?

c What is the setting of the story?

2 Which sentence below is an instruction?

a The rain drips and the rain drops.

b First, break the egg.

c One day, Fox went for a walk.

3 What can you see in each picture? Finish the sentences. Use **and** in each sentence.

| a ball | a bat |

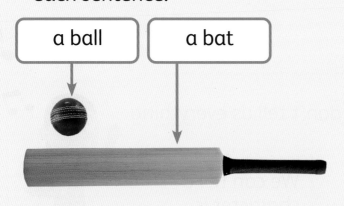

| a spider | a web |

a Here is _____ .

b Here is _____ .

4 Choose the word to complete each instruction. Write the sentence.

   a First, wash/washes your hands.

   b Next, puts/put on an apron.

   c Then, cut/cuts the apple.

5 Look at these words:

   (slip)   (back)   (slop)   (sack)

   a Write the two words that rhyme.

   b Write the two words that start in the same way.

6 Read the sentence.

We have packed our bags and now we are going home.

   a Write the verb that ends in **ing**.

   b Write the verb that ends in **ed**.

117

At home

Learn

Sometimes the words in a story don't tell us everything. We can pick up **clues** from:

- the way a character acts
- the way a character looks.

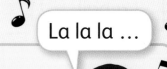
La la la …

We can tell a character is relaxed and happy if they are singing.

Do you remember?

The **setting** is the place where a story happens.

- Stories have many different settings!
- Stories can be set in places you know, like a park, a school or home.

Get started!

The story on page 119 is set in a village in South Africa. A young boy, Shepherd, is getting dressed. He is putting on his tackies – his trainers. It is very noisy in his house. Listen and point.

Not So Fast, Songololo

Listen to the noise!

'Weh, weh, weh!' Uzuti is crying. Adelaide is shouting. 'Mongi, give me back my yellow pen!' Mama calls, 'Shepherd, get up! Come on, Shepherd.' Mr Motiki's dog is barking at someone coming up the road.

Shepherd likes doing things slowly. He sings a little, then he pulls on his T-shirt. He plays a little and then he puts on his shoes – his tackies. They are very old tackies. When they were new, they belonged to Mongi. But now they have holes in them and they belong to Shepherd.

Mr Motiki's dog is still barking at someone coming up the road.

Only an old person walks so slowly. Look how she walks a little and then stops to **lean** on her stick for a while.

Mr Motiki's dog has stopped barking. Instead he is wagging his tail. It's OK. It's only Gogo, Shepherd's granny.

Gogo is old, but her face shines like new shoes. Her hands are large and used to hard work, but when they touch, they are gentle.

By Niki Daly

Glossary
tackies: trainers
lean: put your weight on, rest

1 Imagine your house in the morning. What can you hear? Write a sentence starting: *In the morning, I can hear …*

Can you hear quiet noises like the clock ticking? Can you hear loud noises like your brother or sister shouting?

2 Tell your partner how you know that:

   a Shepherd is happy and relaxed.

   b Shepherd's family is not rich.

   c Mr Motiki's dog knows Gogo.

3 Write the names of three people making a noise in the story.

4 With your partner, pretend to be Shepherd putting on his shoes. Can you show that he is happy and not in a rush?

Can you show how Gogo and Shepherd feel without using words?

5 Pretend to be Gogo walking up the road. Show how tired and old she is.

Go further

1 Listen and point as your teacher rereads the story opening. What do you think will happen next? Tell your partner.

2 Who do you think will be the two main characters in the story?

   a Write their names.

   b Write one sentence about each character.

Do Gogo and Shepherd smile and wave? Do they hug each other?

3 Imagine that Shepherd comes outside to meet Gogo. With your partner, role-play the meeting:

   • What do they say?

   • What do they do?

   Can you show how they feel without words?

4 Write one sentence for each speech bubble to show how Shepherd and Gogo feel when they see each other.

Try and use the word **and** in each sentence.

⭐ **Challenge yourself!**

Write a sentence to show how each character feels in this picture.

Mama

Shepherd

Uzuti

Mongi

Adelaide

Did you know?

Niki Daly was born in Cape Town, South Africa. He is an author and an illustrator. In the past, he was a singer and a songwriter. He has won many prizes for his books including three awards for *Not So Fast, Songololo*.

Niki Daly

121

At the shops

Learn

We can ask **questions** about a story. We can ask questions about a character, a setting or what will happen next.

What does Shepherd want to do?

What is the market like?

Will Gogo buy Shepherd a present?

Do you remember?

We can use **time words** in stories. They help us to know when things happen.
(At first) (Then) (Next) (Later) (Finally)

Get started!

1 Shepherd has gone to help Gogo with her shopping. Shepherd sees a pair of red **trainers** in the window of a shoe shop and wishes he could buy them. Listen and point to the next part of the story.

In the big shop, Gogo looks at her shopping list. She must buy some **groceries**, a new plastic cloth, a mug, and a bottle to keep beans in. Everything costs so much money. Gogo keeps her money in a little bag that she pins to the inside of her **sleeve**. There it is always safe.

Now it's time to cross that busy road again. Hey! There's the little **Green Man**.

They pass the flower sellers and a clothes shop. Look! There's the shoe shop with those bright red tackies looking so nice and new. Shepherd presses his nose against the shop window for a last look.

'Come, Songololo!' calls Gogo. Songololo is her special name for her grandson.

Now, see! Instead of **passing by**, Gogo goes straight into the shoe shop. She really does!

Shepherd looks at Gogo's old shoes. They look like worn out tyres on an old car.

'How much are those red tackies in the window?' asks Gogo.

'Four **rands**,' the man **replies**.

'Will you see if they fit the boy?' asks Gogo.

Shepherd takes off his tackies and slowly fits his feet into the new ones. The man presses around his toes.

'They fit him very well,' he says.

2 How does Shepherd feel when:
   a he sees the red tackies?
   b he looks at Gogo's old shoes?
   c he tries on the red tackies?
3 Tell the story so far to your partner. Try and use some of these words:

   (First)   (Then)   (Next)

   (At last)   (Finally)

4 Write some sentences to show what has happened in the story so far using the time words above.

> **Glossary**
> **trainers**: sneakers, plimsolls
> **groceries**: food shopping
> **sleeve**: the arm of a shirt
> **Green Man**: the sign on a road crossing to show it is safe to cross
> **passing by**: walking past
> **rands**: South African money
> **replies**: says

Go further

1 Can you remember a time when you had new shoes? Did you like them? Tell your partner.

2 Write a story about a child who goes to the shops to buy new shoes or new clothes. Plan your story:
   - *Beginning*: Say who is going shopping.
   - *Middle*: Your character sees something they like.
   - *End*: Does your character get the clothes or shoes they want?

3 Draw pictures for your story. Draw:
   - one picture for the **beginning**
   - two or three pictures for the **middle**
   - one picture for the **end**.

Use the pictures to tell your story.

4 Write a sentence for each picture. Try to use these words:

(first) (then) (next)

(at last) (finally)

Remember to use capital letters and full stops.

5 Read your story to a partner.

Challenge yourself!

1 Talk about the character of Gogo with a partner. Ask more questions about Gogo, for example:
   - *Why doesn't Gogo buy herself new shoes?*
   - *Why does Gogo buy shoes for Shepherd?*

2 Draw a picture of Gogo. Write some sentences to describe Gogo's character. For example: *Gogo is kind*.

At the park

Learn

We can read **stories** set in the park or the shops.

Remember we can use **beginning**, **middle** and **end** to plan a story.

Get started!

1   This story is set in the park. Listen and point.

Shark in the Park

Down at the park,
a little boy
is **testing out**
his **brand new** toy.

Timothy Pope, Timothy Pope
is looking through his **telescope**.
He looks at the sky. He looks at the ground.

He looks left and right.
He looks all around.

And this is what he sees.
What a nasty surprise!
In his loudest voice,
Timothy cries,
'THERE'S
A SHARK
IN THE PARK!'

A shark? **Fancy that!**
It's only a cat!

By Nick Sharratt

Glossary

testing out: trying out
brand new: completely new
telescope: a tube that makes far away things look closer
Fancy that!: My goodness!

2 Write the answers.

   a Who is the main character?

   b Where is the story set?

   c Is there a shark in the park?

   d What does Timothy really see?

3 Find these phrases in the poem. Tell your partner what you think they mean.

   (testing out) (brand new) (Fancy that!)

4 This story rhymes. Find and copy a pair of words from the story that rhyme.

5 Talk about your local park with your partner. What do you do there?

6 Copy and complete these sentences. Add two more sentences. Use these words:

   (slide) (spin) (run) (roundabout) (swings) (go)

   (climb) (jump) (dig) (sandpit) (climbing frame)

   a At the park I ＿＿＿＿＿＿ on the ＿＿＿＿＿＿.

   b I like to ＿＿＿＿＿＿ in the ＿＿＿＿＿＿ at the park.

Go further

1 Imagine that Timothy Pope has seen these things through his telescope:

Look at each picture with your partner. What do you think it is?

2 Complete these sentences using your ideas.

a Oh help! What's that? _____.

b Oh no! What's there? I hope it's not a _____.

c Run away! Let's go! _____.

3 Look at these pictures. What has Timothy Pope really seen? Write the words.

4 Plan a story set in the park. Use **beginning**, **middle** and **end** to plan your story. For example:

Beginning	Middle	End
There are lots of children having fun in the park. *Timothy Pope is looking through his telescope.* *He sees something scary.*	*Timothy tells everyone to run away.* *The people in the park panic.*	*Timothy sees that it is not something scary.*

5 Use your plan to tell your story.

6 Write the beginning of your story.

Add two of these time words or phrases to your story:

(There once was)   (One day)   (It was a lovely day)

(Suddenly)   (Then)

⭐ **Challenge yourself!**

1 Write the middle and end of your story.
In the middle of your story, you could say:

• how everyone in the park feels when Timothy shouts

• what everyone does when they panic, for example: *rush*, *push*, *scream* and *run*.

2 Read your story to a partner. Ask them to tell you one thing they like and one thing they think you should change.

> Remember: the **middle** of the story is where most of the story takes place.

Going on an outing

Do you remember?

We can add **s** or **es** to the end of a **noun** to show there is **more than one**.

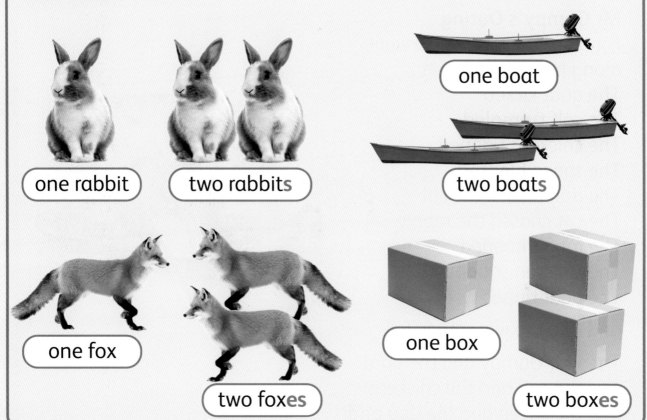

one rabbit

two rabbits

one boat

two boats

one fox

two foxes

one box

two boxes

Learn

Verbs are **doing** words.

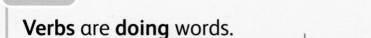

Verbs often end in **s**, **ing** or **ed**. If they end in **ed**, it means that the verb has happened in the past.

The boat rocks.

The boat is rocking.

The boat rocked.

129

Get started!

This story is about an outing that goes wrong. Mr Gumpy goes on a boat trip. As he goes down the river, children and animals ask if they can join him. Mr Gumpy says 'yes' to everyone! Listen and point to find out what happened next.

Mr Gumpy's Outing

For a little while they all went along happily but then …
The goat kicked
The calf **trampled**
The chickens flapped
The sheep **bleated**
The dog teased the cat
The cat chased the rabbit
The rabbit hopped
The children **squabbled**
The boat tipped …

and into the water they fell.

Then Mr Gumpy and the goat and the calf and the chickens and the sheep and the dog and the cat and the rabbit and the children all swam to the **bank** and climbed out to dry in the hot sun.

'We'll walk home across the fields,' said Mr Gumpy. 'It's time for tea.'

By John Burningham

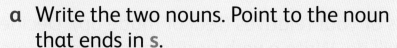

1 Have you ever been on an outing?
   What happened? Discuss with your partner.

2 Look at these words from the story:

chickens   squabbled   tipped   boat

   a Write the two nouns. Point to the noun
      that ends in **s**.

   b Write the two verbs. Point to the letters **ed** in each verb.

3 Imagine an elephant, a fox and a frog went on the boat with
   Mr Gumpy. What did they do? Write the sentences. Choose
   a word for each animal. Use these words:

trumpeted   barked   jumped

stamped   crawled   bounced

   a The elephant _____.
   b The fox _____.
   c The frog _____.

4 Use your sentences to
   tell a partner your own
   story. What happens
   in the end? Start:

   For a little while, they
   all went along happily.
   Then …

Glossary
trampled: crushed (with feet)
bleated: cried (for a goat or a sheep)
squabbled: argued
bank: side of a river

Geography

1 Find out the name of the river that is nearest to where you live.

2 Which towns does it go through? Which animals live in it?

Go further

1 Imagine that you have gone on a boat trip. All your relatives (real or made up) have climbed onto your boat. With a partner, discuss the annoying things your relatives might do on the boat. For example: *shout*, *poke*, *argue*, *sing*, *push* and *dance*.

2 Make a list of names of your relatives (real or made up). Decide what each relative will do. Write a verb beside each name. Here are some useful words:

(Auntie) (cousin) (Uncle) (squabbled) (wriggled) (argued)

(pushed) (rocked) (danced) (jumped) (sang)

3 Write your story. Use this to help you:

For a little while, we went on happily but then _____

_____

_____

and into the water we fell!

We use a capital letter for names, such as **Auntie Aisha** or **Mr Gumpy**.

⭐ Challenge yourself!

1 What happens at the end of your story? Write a few more sentences to say what happens after your relatives fall in the water.

2 Read your story to a partner. Ask them to tell you one thing they like and one thing they think you should change.

At school

If we listen carefully to someone, we will know how they feel.

If we listen carefully to each other, we will work well in a group.

When someone is speaking to you, look at their face. This will help you to understand them better.

Get started!

1   Have you ever had a worry at home or at school? Ruby has a worry. Her worry starts to follow her everywhere. Listen and point.

Ruby's Worry

Ruby loved being Ruby. She loved to swing up high and she loved to **explore** wild, **faraway** places. Sometimes she even went all the way to the very bottom of the garden!

Ruby was **perfectly** happy. Until one day …

… she **discovered** a Worry.

It wasn't a very big Worry.

In fact, it was so small that,

at first, Ruby hardly **noticed** it.

But then the Worry started to grow.

Each day it got a little bit bigger.

It just wouldn't leave her alone.

It was there at breakfast, **staring** at her over the **cereal** box.

And it was STILL there at night when she cleaned her teeth.

The funny thing was that no one else could see – not even her teacher. So Ruby pretended that she couldn't see it either.

By Tom Percival

2 Reread the story with a partner. Look at the picture of Ruby at school. Talk about these questions with a partner.

a Why does the Worry get bigger?

b How does Ruby feel?

c Why has Ruby not drawn on her piece of paper?

d What do you think Ruby should do about her Worry?

e What do you think Ruby might be worrying about? (Has she lost something? Has she forgotten something, perhaps?)

Remember to listen carefully to your partner.

3 Copy and complete these sentences.

a I think Ruby feels _____.

b I think Ruby should _____.

4 Time words tell us when something happened. Find these time phrases in the story:

(Until one day) (Each day) (at breakfast) (at night)

Glossary

explore: go somewhere and look around
faraway: far from home
perfectly: completely

discovered: found
noticed: saw
staring: looking
cereal: breakfast food

Go further

1 Imagine that Ruby is worried about going to the dentist. She is worried that the dentist will know that she has eaten too many sweets.

Work in a group of four.

- In your group, plan the **middle** and **end** of the story in which Ruby goes to the dentist.
- Share your ideas with the group.
- Listen to the other ideas. If the ideas are different, find an idea that everyone is happy with.

> Make sure that the story includes at least one idea from each person in the group.

2 Draw two pictures for the **middle** of the story. Draw one picture for the **end** of the story. Write a sentence for each picture.

> Will Ruby be happy at the end of the story?

Challenge yourself!

Imagine that you are Ruby's friend. You can see that she is worried. Write Ruby a letter.

- You could tell her that we are all worried sometimes.
- You could tell her that you have seen how sad she is.
- You could ask her what is wrong.

Start your letter like this:

> Dear Ruby
>
> I am sorry to hear that you are worried.

Back at the park

Learn

We can use **interesting words** when we write. We can use:

- words that help stories move along

  (Once upon a time) (One day) (Then) (All of a sudden)

- words that we've learned from books we've read

  (tumbled) (shrink) (barely) (hovering)

- words to do with feelings.

  (happy) (sad) (worried)

Do you remember?

We can use **and** to make our sentences longer.

Ruby's Worry sat next to her at breakfast **and** then it followed her to school.

Get started!

1 Ruby's Worry gets bigger and bigger. Find out what happens when she goes to the park. Listen and point. Look out for interesting words.

Remember to use the glossary to find out the meaning of new words.

Glossary
unexpected: surprising
noticed: saw
hovering: floating
realised: found out
shrink: get smaller
tumbled: fell
barely: hardly

Then one day, something **unexpected** happened …

Ruby **noticed** a boy sitting alone at the park.

He looked how she felt – sad.

And then she noticed something else, something **hovering** next to him. Could it be a Worry?

Ruby **realised** that she wasn't the only person with a Worry after all.

Other people had them too.

She asked the boy what was on his mind and as he told her, the strangest thing happened …

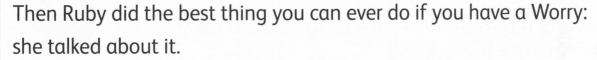

his Worry began to **shrink**!

Then Ruby did the best thing you can ever do if you have a Worry:

she talked about it.

As the words **tumbled** out, Ruby's Worry began to shrink until it was **barely** there at all.

Soon both of their Worries were gone!

By Tom Percival

2 Reread the story with your partner. Answer these questions together:

   a How did Ruby know that the boy had a Worry?

   b Why did the Worries get smaller?

3 Find these words in the story. Tell your partner what they mean.

   (tumbled) (shrink) (hovering) (unexpected)

   With your partner, write a new sentence for each word.

Go further

1 a Retell the story to a partner. Think of questions you would like to ask the boy, for example:

- *What is your name?*
- *Where did you find your Worry?*
- *Did the Worry follow you around?*
- *How did you feel at school?*
- *How did you feel when you talked to Ruby?*

b Make up answers for the boy.

2 Draw a story for the boy. For example:

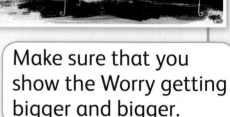

Make sure that you show the Worry getting bigger and bigger.

- **Beginning:** *He finds his Worry.*
- **Middle:** *His Worry follows him around.*
- **End:** *He meets Ruby and tells her his Worry.*

3 Write a sentence for each picture in the story. Try to use these words:

(Once upon a time) (One day) (hovering) (shrink)

(The next day) (and) (worried) (sad) (felt)

4 Share your story with your partner. Read their story. Tell your partner what you like about their story. Tell them one thing that they could do to improve their story.

Challenge yourself!

Make a *What to do if you have a Worry* poster for the classroom. Write down the people that we can talk to, for example:

(parents) (carers) (brothers or sisters) (grandparents)

(friends) (teachers)

At home again

Do you remember?

We can tell how someone is feeling.

- We can listen to what they say.
- We can see the look on their face.
- We can see how they behave.

> Listen carefully to your friends so that you know how they feel.

Get started!

1 Katie Morag is not happy. Her mother, Mrs McColl, has just had a new baby and Katie Morag feels left out. Listen and point.

Katie Morag and the Tiresome Ted

There was great excitement on the **Isle** of Struay. Mrs McColl at the Post Office had had a new baby, and everyone was **delighted**.

Everyone, that is, except Katie Morag. She had been in a bad mood ever since the new baby had arrived.

'No one talks to me anymore,' she **grumbled** to herself, 'or brings me presents.'

'Don't worry,' everyone said **knowingly**. 'Katie Morag will soon get over it.'

But Katie Morag could not and would not get over it. She kept doing naughty things, like stamping her feet and **nipping** her little brother, Liam.

One day she was so cross that she **stomped** all the way to the **jetty** and kicked her friendly old one-eyed teddy bear into the sea.

'**Tiresome Ted**!' she shouted, as he disappeared into the **choppy** waves.

By Mairi Hedderwick

2 Tell a partner how Katie Morag feels.

3 a Look at this list of verbs. Which four verbs are things that Katie does? Write the verbs.

(stomped) (shouted) (helped) (smiled) (grumbled)

(laughed) (kicked)

b Point to the **ed** ending in each verb.

4 a Pretend to be Katie Morag. With a partner, take turns to pretend to:

- rumble
- stamp
- pinch
- kick.

b Can you show how cross and upset Katie Morag is?

Remember you are just pretending!

5 Imagine that Katie Morag is *happy* about the baby. Copy and complete these sentences.

(laughing) (glad) (singing)

Katie Morag was so happy about the baby. She kept _____ and _____. She was _____ to have a little sister.

Have you read any other Katie Morag stories?

Glossary

isle: island

delighted: very happy

grumbled: complained

knowingly: showing that they have seen children behave like this before

nipping: pinching

stomped: walked crossly

jetty: an area for boats to tie up

tiresome: irritating

Ted: the name of her toy

choppy: with lots of waves

Go further

1 Discuss with your partner about a time you felt angry or upset. Tell your partner how you behaved.

2 What makes you happy? What makes you angry? What makes you sad? Copy and complete these sentences.

   a I feel _____ when _____.

   b I feel _____ when _____.

   c I feel _____ when _____.

3 Remember what helped Ruby with her Worry. What could Katie Morag do? Think of some ideas with a partner.

> Katie Morag should cuddle the baby.

> Katie Morag should talk to her mother.

4 Write a letter to Katie Morag telling her what she should do. Start your letter like this:

> Dear Katie Morag
>
> I am sorry that you feel sad and cross. I think you should …

Challenge yourself!

1 Look at the **verbs** in the boxes. With a partner, talk about the meaning of each word. What feeling does each action show?

(cried) (frowned) (sobbed) (shouted) (kicked)

(sulked) (moaned) (whispered) (stomped)

(laughed) (grinned) (skipped) (jumped)

2 Choose your two favourite verbs from the list. Write a sentence for each word. For example:

> Alfie sulked as he walked home with Gran.

> Suki frowned as she walked onto the stage.

3 Write the missing word to show how Katie Morag feels.

cross   happy   funny   scared   sleepy

a Katie Morag was _____. She skipped across the room.

b Katie Morag was _____. She dragged her feet as she walked.

c Katie Morag was _____. She tiptoed across the room.

Did you know?

The story *Katie Morag and the Tiresome Ted* is set on the Isle of Struay. It is based on the real Scottish island of Coll. The author Mairi Hedderwick lives on Coll. There are several Katie Morag stories all about her adventures!

What can you do?

Read and review what you can do.
- ✔ I can say where a story is set.
- ✔ I can say how a character feels.
- ✔ I can ask questions about a story.
- ✔ I can use **beginning**, **middle** and **end** to plan a story.
- ✔ I can add **s** or **es** to a noun.
- ✔ I can read verbs ending in **ing**, **ed** or **s**.
- ✔ I can look at someone when they are talking.
- ✔ I can use interesting words when I write.
- ✔ I can use **and** to make a sentence longer.

Now you have read stories with different settings.

Bengal Tiger

We can talk about the **syllables** in a word.

Say the words and clap the **syllables**.

- **caterpillar** has four syllables:

  cat-er-pil-lar

- **gorilla** has three syllables:

  go-ril-la

- **tiger** has two syllables:

  ti-ger

Get started!

1 What is your favourite animal?

- Draw the animal, clap the syllables and write its name.

- Say how many syllables are in the name.

- With three friends, take turns to say and clap your animal's name. Repeat a few times.

Well done! You have made up a poem!

Try and join some of your letters.

Get started!

2 Listen and point to this animal poem.

Bengal Tiger

We are the Bengal Tigers,
Our teeth are sharp like daggers.
We are not good climbers,
But we are good swimmers.

Our memory is sharp.
And we like to **hunt** in the dark.

If our prey is on a bark,
And our hunger demands the work,
We will climb that bark!

We don't have **similarities**,
For stripe patterns are our **peculiarities**.

We are the national animal of India.
We are the national pride of India!

By Prithviraj Shirole

3 Find and copy:
- two words in the poem that rhyme with **shark**
- an adjective that is also a type of knife
- a word that means 'to go up a tree':

4 Clap and count the syllables in these words:

(tiger) (kangaroo) (armadillo)

Glossary

hunt: to chase something to catch it

similarities: things that are the same

peculiarities: unusual features

Go further

Choose animals to write and complete the poem.

hippo rhino
rhino hippo

_____ _____

_____

_____

_____

_____

Choose two: beetle / penguin / hedgehog

Choose one: moose / stoat

Choose one: grumpy camel / snowy owl

Choose one: fluffy mammal / guinea fowl

Choose one: goose / goat

Choose one: butterfly / elephant

⭐ Challenge yourself!

1 Use these animal names and phrases to write a poem.

goat – stoat

grouse – mouse

goose – moose

racoon – baboon

These names have the same number of syllables. That makes the rhyme sound strong.

2 Say your poem and clap the syllables in the words. Can you make it better?

More animals

Learn

We can use **adjectives** to describe what things are like:

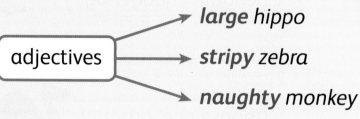

adjectives → **large** *hippo*

→ **stripy** *zebra*

→ **naughty** *monkey*

Get started!

1   This poem tells a silly story. Join in and point.

The Animal Fair

We went to the animal fair,
The birds and beasts were there.
The big baboon
By the light of the moon
Was combing his **auburn hair**.
The monkey fell out of his **bunk**
And slipped down the elephant's trunk.
The elephant sneezed
And fell on his knees.
But what became of the monkey
Monkey, monkey
Monkey, monkey?

Anonymous

What do you think happened to the monkey?

2 Find words that rhyme in the poem on page 146.

3 Talk about these questions with your partner:

    a Who is the main character?

    b Why did the elephant sneeze?

    c Why did the monkey disappear?

4 Write the adjective in each sentence.

    a The big baboon.

    b The baboon had long hair.

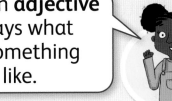

An **adjective** says what something is like.

5 Write the verb in each sentence.

    a The baboon combed his hair.

    b The elephant sneezes.

    c The monkey fell.

A **verb** often ends in **ed**, **ing** or **s**.

6 Use these pictures to tell the story in the poem with your partner.

7 Write a sentence for each picture above. Use these words from the poem:

(baboon) (moon) (combing)

(sneezed) (knees) (zoomed)

Glossary

auburn hair: red-gold coloured hair

bunk: two beds placed on top of each other

Go further

1 Imagine a trip to the zoo. Tell your partner what you can see, hear and smell.

> What silly things are the animals doing?

2 a Write a list animals who live in the zoo.

b Write an adjective to go with each animal. Write your list of animals as a poem For example:

> Look at pictures of animals to help you.

stripy zebra
black panther
cheeky monkey
sleepy sloth

Challenge yourself!

Write a second verse for your poem.

- Write another list of animals.

- Now write a verb ending in **ing** to go with each animal. Here are some words to help you:

prowling   crawling   swimming

laughing   cruising   snapping

Global Perspectives Challenge: Working and having a job

Find out about the jobs that people do at a zoo. Tell your class or a group what you have found out.

Snap, Snap!

Learn

We can talk loudly. We can talk quietly.

We can use our voices in different ways to make a poem fun to listen to.

We can collect interesting words when we read. We can use these words in our own writing.

Write any words that you want to remember in your *Spelling log*.

Get started!

1 Listen and point to these poems about a crocodile. Notice how your teacher uses their voice to make the poem fun to listen to.

Crocodile

When animals come to the
river to drink
I watch for a minute or two
It's such a delight
To **behold** such a sight
That I can't **resist chomping**
a few.

By Giles Andreae

Glossary

behold: see   **resist**: stop myself   **chomping**: eating

149

The Crocodile

How **doth** the little crocodile
    Improve his shining tail,
And pour the waters of the **Nile**
    On every golden **scale**!
How cheerfully he seems to **grin**,
    How neatly spreads his claws,
And welcomes little fishes in,
    With gently smiling jaws!

By Lewis Carroll

2 Find a rhyming word in the poems for each word. Write the pairs.

(two) (delight) (crocodile) (tail)

3 Write the answer to these questions about the first poem.

a *I watch for a minute or two.* Who is talking?
- a crocodile
- a fish
- a hunter

b *I can't resist chomping a few.* What happens to the animals?
- They are photographed.
- They are eaten.
- They are left alone.

c Why is the crocodile pleased to see the animals in the second poem?
- He thinks they are pretty.
- They are his friends.
- He wants to eat them.

> **Glossary**
> **doth**: does
> **improve**: make better
> **Nile**: a river in Africa
> **scale**: part of a crocodile's skin
> **grin**: smile

4 Work with a partner on a performance of the first poem. Say the ending like a secret. Make the poem fun to listen to.

Go further

1 Create a performance of *The Crocodile* by Lewis Carroll. Can you:
    • make the words **shiny** and **golden** sound exciting?
    • show that the crocodile is going to eat the fish?
    • smile like a crocodile as you read the poem?

2 Find these interesting words in the two poems:

(delight) (chomping) (shining) (golden)

(neatly) (welcomes) (Nile)

Write the words in your *Spelling log*.

3 Draw a picture of the crocodile from the second poem. Write sentences to describe it using some of the interesting words from your *Spelling log*.

Challenge yourself!

1 Find words in the poems that mean:
    a eating
    b happy thing
    c make better
    d happily

2 Write your own poem about a crocodile. Here are some words to help you:

(smiling) (welcomes) (fish)

(chomping) (jaws)

(hungry) (eat)

Did you know?

• Crocodiles are the largest reptiles on Earth.
• They live in Africa, Asia, Australia and America.
• They have very sharp teeth and have the strongest bite of any animal.
• They stay completely still for hours but can attack quickly.

Incy Wincy Spider

We can present our work in different ways.
- We can write clearly to create a good impression.
- We can use a computer.
- We can write beautifully for a display.
- We can use different colours.
- We can use different text sizes.

> When we form our letters correctly, other people can read what we write.

Get started!

1 Join in and point to these spider poems.

Incy Wincy Spider

Incy Wincy Spider
Went up the **water spout**
Down came the rain and
Washed the spider out
Out came the sun and
Dried up all the rain
So, Incy Wincy spider went
Up the spout again …

Anonymous

The Climber

See him climbing up the wall,
Step by step I watch him crawl,
Leg by leg he feels his way
Through the shadow of the day.
At the ceiling he will stop,
Cast his **threads** and start to drop
Down and down, he knows no **failure**,
Expert climber and **abseiler**.

Coral Rumble

2 Reread *Incy Wincy Spider* with a partner. Talk about what happens to the spider.

3 Draw three pictures to show what happened at the beginning, the middle and the end of the poem.

4 Reread *The Climber* with a partner. Talk about what happens in the poem.

5 Find these words in *The Climber*. Read the line. Tell your partner what they mean.

> step by step   leg by leg   through the shadow

6 Find the words in the poem that rhyme with these words:

a wall
b failure
c stop
d way

Do you think the spider is climbing slowly or quickly? Why?

Are the rhyming parts of these words spelled the same?
Tell your partner.

7 Choose a poem from page 152 to read again. Tell a partner why you like it.

Incy Wincy Spider

The Climber

Glossary

water spout: drain pipe
cast: throw
threads: small pieces of a spider's web

failure: going wrong
expert: very good
abseiler: someone who can use a rope to jump down a cliff

Go further

1 Work in a group. Look at this photograph.

- In your group, describe the spider.
- Write the word or words neatly on pieces of card. Can you join some letters?

> I think spiders are **creepy**, **scary** and **hairy**.

> I think spiders are **shy**, **strong** and **clever**.

2 With your group, draw a large spider's web. Hang your words or sentences like spiders from the web.

Challenge yourself!

1 Look at other poems about spiders. Choose your favourite.

2 Copy the poem for display using your best handwriting. Think of interesting ways to present the poem.

3 Look at all your spider webs in the classroom. Copy words you like. Look at the words you have written. Do any of them go well together? Use the words to write a spider poem. Here is an example:

creepy	strong
hairy	sticky
scary	secret
dangerous	strong
eek SPIDER	eek SPIDER'S WEB

Science

Find out facts about spiders.

- Where do they live?
- What do they eat?
- What types of spiders are in your country?

My animal poem

Do you remember?

When we want to **spell** a **new word**, we:
- say the word slowly to hear each sound
- write the letters for each sound
- ask for help.

Many words that **rhyme** have similar spelling patterns.

(claw – paw) (delight – sight) (moose – goose)

Learn

A **list poem** is a poem that is a list of items.
Do you remember this list poem?

stripy zebras
black panther
cheeky monkey
sleepy sloth

Get started!

1 A list poem can be very short! Read this list poem with a partner.

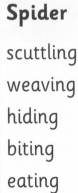

Spider

scuttling
weaving
hiding
biting
eating

2 Look at the words in the poem. Are they nouns, adjectives or adverbs?

3 Which poem in Unit 8 is your favourite? Tell your partner why.

4 Look at the words in **bold** in these lines from poems. Talk to your partner about why these verbs end in **s**.

> The words in a list poem often match. In this poem, they are all verbs ending in **ing**.

> We all like different poems.

She **lights up** the sky.　　He **spreads** his claws.　　She **feels** her way.

5 These words all come from the poems you have read in this unit. With a partner, write the words onto separate pieces of card.

cat　　monkey　　moose　　elephant　　goat

gorilla　　zebra　　tiger　　spider　　giraffe

walks　　climbs　　eats　　laughs　　munches

hunts　　creeps　　thumps　　trumpets　　weaves

6 Sort the cards into pairs of animals and verbs that go well together. Try out different pairs of words.

gorilla	thumps
cat	creeps
spider	weaves

7 Use the cards to create a list poem. Take a photograph of your poem.

> A poem does not need to rhyme.

monkey	laughs
goat	climbs
zebra	eats
elephant	trumpets

Go further

1   Look at your list poem from *Get started!* Now muddle up the words. Add new cards for these words:

(jumps)   (smells)   (pads)   (growls)   (prowls)

(waits)   (sleeps)   (crawls)   (grumps)

2   Make a new poem using the words from question 1.

3   Can you write other animal names that go with the ones on the cards? Here are some examples:

- (gorilla – chinchilla)

- (moose – goose)

- (tiger – spider)

- (goat – stoat)

Choose animal names that rhyme or share sounds at the beginning or the middle.

Use phonics to spell the new animal name.

4   Write your animal names as a list poem like this:

There are:
gorillas and chinchillas
goats and stoats
a moose and a goose

Challenge yourself!

1 Look at your animal poem. Add an adjective (a describing word) to each animal name. Use the word to make your lines longer. Write your new, longer poem. For example:

> *Big gorillas and soft chinchillas*
> *Silly goats and little stoats*
> *Huge moose and a fluffy goose.*

Big, **soft** and **silly** are all adjectives.

You can make your poem as long as you like!

2 Read your poem aloud.

- Can you make some lines better?
- Can you choose better adjectives?

3 Talk to your partner about how you wrote your poem. Listen to their poem and ask them questions.

What can you do?

Read and review what you can do.

- ✔ I can clap the syllables in a word.
- ✔ I can talk about a poem I have read and say which poems I like.

Now you have read some fun animal poems.

- ✔ I can find verbs, nouns and adjectives in poems.
- ✔ I can use my voice in different ways to make a poem sound interesting when I read it aloud.
- ✔ I can collect interesting words in a *Spelling log*.
- ✔ I can write neatly so that my work looks attractive.
- ✔ I can write neatly so that my words are easy to read.
- ✔ I can point out words that rhyme with the same spelling pattern.

Reduce, reuse, recycle

Learn

There is information all around us.

We can find information in books, in posters, on labels and on the internet.

Information texts are about the real world.

An information text may look like this:

REDUCE REUSE RECYCLE

There are small things we can do to become greener. Try these:

- Use less plastic.
- Use a refillable bottle.
- Turn off lights when you're not in the room.
- Walk or cycle if you can instead of using a car or bus.

Make sure you recycle waste paper.

Fact: Old batteries can poison the soil. You should recycle your batteries at your local shop!

Heading

A word to help us to know what we can read about.

Main text

The most important information

Caption

A sentence about a picture.

Fact box

An extra interesting fact.

159

Get started!

Can you see any posters in your classroom?

1 Read this poster about recycling.
   Point to these things in the information text:

   a a heading **b** a picture

   c a caption **d** a fact box

Reduce, reuse, recycle

We throw away too much **rubbish**.
This **rubbish harms** our world.

How can we throw away less? We can …

Reduce

Try not to buy plastic bags and bottles.

Remember to take a bag with you to the shops.

Reuse

Use lunch boxes and **refillable** bottles.

Write on both sides of the paper.

Use the same shopping bag many times.

Recycle

Sort out your rubbish.
Recycle as much as you can.

60 million plastic bottles are thrown away every day!

Food

Paper and card

Bottles and cans

Food

Food waste can be turned into compost for the garden.

2 Read the poster again with your partner. Discuss with your partner what you know about recycling.

3 Answer these questions about the poster:

  a What sort of text is this?

  (story) (poem) (information)

  b Where can you find out about 60 million plastic bottles?

  (picture) (fact box) (heading)

  c Find and copy a caption.

4 Match the word to its meaning. Write the missing word.

  (reuse) (recycle) (reduce)

  a _____ : to use something again

  b _____ : to make or use less

  c _____ : to put rubbish in a bin where it can be sent somewhere to be made into something new

5 Use the poster to ask your partner a question.

  a Tell your partner to show where they found the answer.

  b Think of two questions you have about recycling. Can you find the answers in an information book?

> Remember to look carefully at the poster to answer the question.

Glossary

rubbish: something we want to throw away

harms: hurts

reduce: to make or use less

reuse: to use something again

refillable: can be filled again

recycle/recycling: to send rubbish away to be turned into something else

Go further

1 Go on a poster hunt in your school or classroom.

2 Make a poster to tell learners in your school to recycle their rubbish. Think about the best posters you have seen. What will yours include?

- a heading
- a picture
- a fact box
- a caption.

Put the **recycling logo** on your poster. It looks like this:

Did you know?

- It takes 450 years for a plastic bottle to break down.
- There are billions of plastic bottles and bags in oceans.
- Animals in the ocean try to eat plastic bottles and bags, and this can make them very sick.
- Some birds and sea animals get tangled in plastic nets and bags.
- Nearly every piece of plastic ever made still exists on Earth.

Challenge yourself!

1 Reread the poster on page 160 and the information above.

2 Create a poster to tell people to buy less plastic. Tell people:

- why plastic is bad for the Earth
- what people can do instead of buying plastic.

3 Read your poster to a partner. Check it has: a heading, a fact box, a picture and a caption.

Display your poster in the classroom.

Information books

Do you remember?

An **information book** tells you facts about the world and how things work.

Learn

An **information book** has these things to help you find the information you need.

Title

The title tells you what the book is about.

Our Planet

Find out more about our planet! Do you know how many types of animals there are? Can you guess how many people live on the planet? Read lots of cool facts inside.

Blurb

The blurb is found on the back cover of a book. It tells you about the book.

Heading This tells you what a part of the book is about.

Subheading

This tells you what a smaller part of the book is about.

Contents

This tells you where you can find information in the book.

Contents

People and the planet

Where do all the people live?

Some people live in big cities like New York.

Caption

A caption tells you about a picture.

Get started!

1 Look at the information text below. Point to a:

(main heading) (subheading) (picture) (caption)

2 Read these sentences with a partner. Copy the sentence that best matches the information in the text.

a The oceans are beautiful places with wonderful animals.

b Plastic in the oceans harms birds and sea animals.

c We must all recycle as much plastic as we can.

Plastic in the oceans

Plastic bags, bottles and rubbish have been washed into the sea.

Sea birds

Sea birds and their chicks eat plastic rubbish washed up on islands. This can kill them.

Tangled up

Turtles can get caught in plastic bags. Huge whales can be tangled in old fishing nets.

62

A plastic bag has been found at the very bottom of the ocean.

63

---

3 *Huge whales can be **tangled** in old fishing nets.*
What does the word **tangled** mean?

a tied up   b have fun

c chased

4 Write a sentence about plastic in the ocean.

Have you read other information books? What were they about?

Glossary

tangled: caught up in something like a rope or a net

Go further

1 Tell a partner what each of these books might be about.

 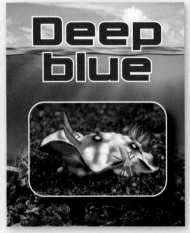 

2 Match the title of each book to its blurb below. Write the title.

   a What is hurting sea birds? Find out in this book.

   b Read about the strange animals at the bottom of the sea.

   c Learn about the things that can be made from plastic.

3 Which of the books would you like to read? Tell your partner. Explain why.

★ Challenge yourself!

1 Read this contents page. Discuss it with a partner. What do you think each chapter will be about?

2 Write a caption for this picture.

CONTENTS

1 Marvellous plastic 2

2 Plastic in the oceans 4

3 Reduce plastics 6

4 Reusing plastics 8

5 A new life for plastics 10

Helpful headings

Learn

Headings can help us find our way around a text.

- They can tell us what we are going to read.
- They can help us find the information that we want.

> A **main heading** will start a chapter.
> A **subheading** is about a small section of text.

Subheading

Recycling ← Main heading

What can we recycle?

Recycling is good for the planet.
We can recycle:
- paper
- cardboard
- plastic
- glass
- aluminium.

Do you remember?

We can join letters that make one sound:

ow   ew   ar   er

Get started!

1 Read the information about recycling on the next page. How many headings and subheadings can you find?

2 Write the answers.

a What is the main heading?

b Write one subheading.

c What clothes can be made from recycled bottles?

d Look at the fact box. Write one thing that recycling plastic saves.

3 Find and discuss the answers with a partner:

a What two types of furniture can be made from recycled bottles?

b How many bottles does it take to make a jumper?

c Why is it good to recycle bottles?

Can you join some of your letters and words?

A new life for plastics

Recycled bottles and bags can be melted down and made into new plastic objects.

Furniture

Playground **equipment** and park benches are made from recycled plastic.

Clothes

T-shirts and jumpers can be made from recycled bottles.

New bottles

Old bottles can be made into new shampoo bottles.

This jumper was made from 60 bottles!

When we recycle plastic, we save:

- oil needed for new plastic
- electricity needed for new plastic
- space in a rubbish dump.

Glossary

furniture: tables, chairs, sofas, benches

equipment: the things we use

Go further

1   This page is missing its subheadings.
    Write a subheading for each space.

2   Write a new section about using a bottle for a craft project.

    a   Write a heading.

    b   Write a sentence about using bottles for crafts.

    c   Draw a picture of a reused bottle.

    d   Write a caption.

A bottle could be made into a pencil pot, a plant pot or a toy rocket!

Plastic everywhere

Plastic is very useful but it needs to be thrown away safely.

Plastic that is not thrown away properly can be washed into the sea.

Plastic in the oceans can harm animals. They can eat it or get tangled in it.

Make sure you put any plastic in the recycling bin.

Remember to join some of your letters and words.

Challenge yourself!

Find out more about recycling, such as *where bottles go* or *how many bottles are recycled*.

• Write a fact box using the information.

• Give your fact box a heading.

Did you know?

Across the world, one million plastic bottles are bought every minute!

Pictures and diagrams

Learn

An information book often has **diagrams**.

A **diagram** is a simple picture that helps us to understand something.

Labels and **captions** help us to understand the diagram better.

labels

Only four out of ten bottles are recycled.

Six out of ten plastic bottles are thrown away.

caption → This picture shows you how many bottles are recycled.

Get started!

1 Read the labels on this picture. What is this picture about? Tell a partner.

Rubbish is blown from a **rubbish dump** into the river and the sea.

The river takes the rubbish to the sea.

A plastic bottle is blown into a river.

A plastic bag falls into a **drain**.

The drain takes the rubbish to the sea.

Glossary

drain: a pipe that takes water away

rubbish dump: a place where rubbish is buried

169

Get started!

2 Work in a group of four. Look at the picture. Point out:
  - a whale in trouble
  - plastic being blown away in the wind
  - plastic in the river
  - a plastic bag going down the drain.

3 Read the labels again. Answer these questions. Write two ideas.

   a How can we stop plastic getting into the sea?

   b How can we clear up the rubbish that is there?

Listen to each other.

Take turns to speak and do not interrupt.

4 Draw a new picture to show your ideas for:
  - stopping plastic from reaching the ocean
  - clearing up plastic.

   Write labels. Remember, your picture needs to be simple and clear.

5 Write a caption to explain your picture.

Remember to join some of your letters and words.

Go further

1 Talk with a partner about what is happening in each picture.

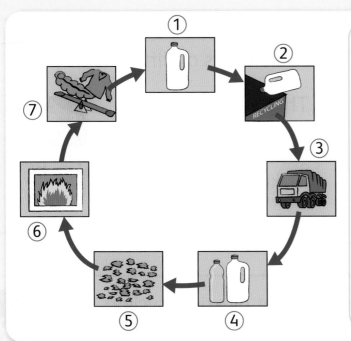

1 An empty bottle.
2 The bottle is put in the recycling bin.
3 The recycling is taken to a recycling centre.
4 The bottles are sorted.
5 The bottles are broken into little pieces.
6 The little pieces are melted.
7 The melted plastic is made into new objects.

2 Write a sentence explaining what the diagram shows you.

3 Write a heading for the diagram.

Challenge yourself!

1 Read what can happen to a plastic bag:

① The plastic bag is thrown away.
② The plastic bag is at the rubbish dump.
③ The wind blows the bag away from the dump.

④ The bag blows into a river.
⑤ The river takes the bag to the sea.
⑥ The bag is eaten by a sea turtle.

2 Draw a diagram to show what happens to the bag. Add a heading and these labels to your diagram.

(bag)   (dump)   (river)   (sea turtle)

My mini-book

Do you remember?

Information books show information in lots of different ways:

- contents page
- headings
- pictures and diagrams
- labels and captions
- fact boxes.

These features help us to find what we are looking for.

Get started!

Make your own information book about plastic recycling.

1 Fold two pieces of A4 paper in half together to create a mini-book. Write numbers on the bottom of each page of the book.

Put number 1 on the front page.

2 On page 1, write the title and draw a picture to show what the book is about. You could use this title: **All about recycling**

All about recycling

3 On page 2, write a heading and a list to show what is in your mini-book. It could look like this:

Contents

4 On page 3, write this heading and add some sentences with information about the problems of plastics.

> Plastic everywhere

You could write about these things:

- The problems of plastic at sea
- How plastic is dangerous to some animals
- How plastic doesn't disappear unless it is recycled.

Look back at the texts you have read in this unit for ideas.

Go further

1 On page 4, write this heading: > Reduce and reuse plastic

2 Draw a picture and write some sentences. Add a caption to your picture.

You could write about these things:

- Reusing shopping bags
- Reusing water bottles
- Not using plastic sandwich bags.

Can you join some of your letters and words?

3 On page 5, write this heading: > Recycle plastic

Write about how plastic can be recycled into something else. Choose something from the list below or use your own ideas. Draw a picture and write some sentences.

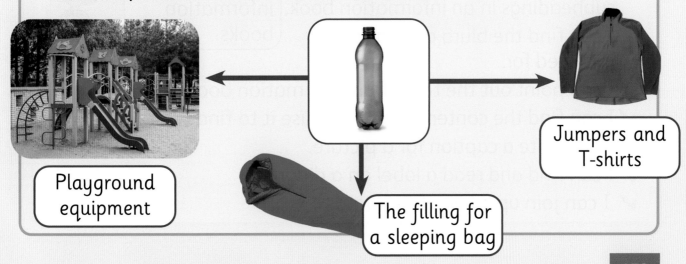

Playground equipment

The filling for a sleeping bag

Jumpers and T-shirts

★ Challenge yourself!

1 Draw and label a diagram on pages 6 and 7 of your mini-book to show how a glass bottle is recycled. Use these labels.

| The bottle is finished. | The bottle is thrown in the recycling bin. |

| The bin lorry collects the recycling and takes it to the recycling plant. | The bottle is sorted at the recycling plant. |

| The bottle is shredded into tiny pieces. | The shredded bottle is melted. | The melted bottle is made into a new object. |

2 Add a blurb to the back of your book.
3 Ask your partner to read your book and say:
- what they like about it.
- one thing that could improve it.

What can you do?

Read and review what you can do.
- ✔ I can find headings and subheadings in an information book.
- ✔ I can find the blurb and say what it is used for.
- ✔ I can point out the title of an information book.
- ✔ I can find the contents page and use it to find information.
- ✔ I can write a caption for a picture.
- ✔ I can find and read a label on a diagram.
- ✔ I can join up some of my words.

Now you know all about information books.

Quiz 3

1 Which of these story settings could you find in real life?

a    b    c

2 Copy and complete the table with these words. An example has been done for you.

(shoes)   (jumping)   (rested)   (singing)   (bus)

(house)   (shouted)   (teacher)   (walking)

Verbs	Nouns
singing	*bus*

3 Look at these words. Write pairs of words that rhyme.

(quick)   (out)   (stoat)   (goat)

(shout)   (fishes)   (dishes)   (stick)

4 Choose the correct word to complete each sentence.
   a We saw three boats / boates on the ocean.
   b We have new recycling bins / bines at school.
   c The plastic bags get stuck in the bushs / bushes.
   d The baby foxs / foxes played in the snow.

5 Choose a subheading to go with each set of information.

(Reduce) (Reuse) (Recycle)

a (_____)

Plastic bottles can be used again and again. We can refill our bottles or reuse plastic boxes.

b (_____)

Plastic bottles can be melted down and made into new items. They can be made into furniture or jumpers.

c (_____)

The best thing we can do for the world is to stop buying plastic bottles. In this way, there will be less plastic everywhere.

6 Look at these covers. Write **information book** or **storybook** for each one.

ⓐ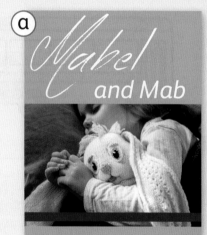

ⓑ

ⓒ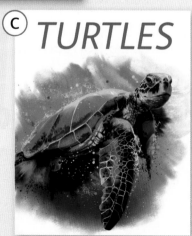

ⓓ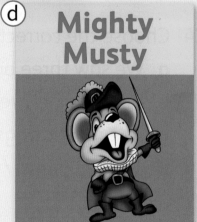